# The Prescott Proposals

## BY HOWARD LINDSAY
## & RUSSEL CROUSE

"Mr. Lindsay and Mr. Crouse, liberals and gentlemen, have found room here and there to say something heartening about the value of the U. N. to the world . . . As a melodrama, it is an exciting piece of work with a lot of suspense."

BROOKS ATKINSON, *New York Times*

"It has bigness, daring, coincidence and neatness . . . You gasp with suspense as a character moves toward a telltale door, or are carried away by a shamelessly heroic appeal for trust in the goodness of mankind."

WILLIAM HAWKINS,
*New York World-Telegram & Sun*

"They have written exactly the sort of play appropriate to two expert and liberal-minded technicians of the American theatre as it is today. They have a sparkling new gimmick for their setting — one of the subcommittees of the United Nations at work. They have an atmosphere of tenseness evolving from a dead body and hints of blackmailed secrecy. For their glamorous, mature heroine they have evolved a romantic interlude long past and a pregnant new interest in a powerful commentator."

*Washington Post*

# The PRESCOTT PROPOSALS

By HOWARD LINDSAY
and RUSSEL CROUSE

 RANDOM HOUSE · NEW YORK

52422

Photographs by Vandamm

TO ANNA

THE PRESCOTT PROPOSALS was first presented by Leland Hayward at the Broadhurst Theatre on the evening of December 16, 1953, with the following cast:


(IN ORDER OF APPEARANCE)

MARY PRESCOTT      Katharine Cornell
    U.N. Delegate from the United States

KATHLEEN MURRAY      Emily Lawrence
    Secretary to Mrs. Prescott

EMMA      Helen Ray

ELLIOTT CLARK      Lorne Greene

JAN CAPEK      Bartlett Robinson
    U.N. Delegate from Czechoslovakia

SIR AUDLEY MARRIOTT      Felix Aylmer
    U.N. Ambassador from the United Kingdom

PAUL-EMILE D'ARCEAU      Roger Dann
    U.N. Delegate from France

DR. ALI MASOUD      Minoo Daver
    U.N. Delegate from Pakistan

ALEXIS PETROVSKY      Ben Astar
    U.N. Delegate from the Soviet Union

MIGUEL FERNANDEZ      Edward Groag
    Conference Officer

ALAN DRAPER      Robert M. Culp
    Press Attache

MIROSLAV BABICKA      Boris Tumarin
    U.N. Alternate Delegate from Czechoslovakia

RUSSIAN AIDE      Jan de Ruth

BRITISH AIDE      J. P. Wilson

PRECIS-WRITER      John Drew Devereaux

Experts and Aides to the United Nations Delegates: Bijou
Fernandez, Joe Masteroff, John Leslie, Sheppard Kerman,
Richard Bengali, Ward Costello, Bernard Reines, Hubert
Beck

*Directed by* Howard Lindsay

*Settings by* Donald Oenslager

*Costumes by* Main Bocher

## SCENES

### ACT ONE

Mary Prescott's apartment.

### ACT TWO

Scene  I. A committee room at the United Nations—
the next afternoon.
Scene II. Mary Prescott's apartment—that night.

### ACT THREE

A committee room at the United Nations—
the next afternoon.

The time is late Autumn.

ACT ONE

# ACT ONE

TIME: *Late autumn. At dusk.*

SCENE: *The living room in the apartment of* MRS. MARY PRESCOTT. *It is situated on the ground floor of a converted brownstone house in a quiet block in the East Sixties in New York City. The entrance from the outside is a door offstage right, which admits into a narrow hall. Offstage left, down the hall, are doors to the bedroom and kitchen, etc. One comes into the living room through a large arch upstage center. In the left wall, downstage, there is a door admitting directly to the bedroom. In the right wall are the two conventional windows overlooking the street.*

*The apartment is furnished in conservative good taste. On the right side of the room is a large desk, for this room serves* MRS. PRESCOTT *both as living room and workroom. On the desk are two telephones and books, reports, correspondence, clippings, etc., giving evidence of constant and busy use. There is a low desk lamp, also a tray of tea things. The desk chair is on the right of the desk. There is another chair left of the desk. On the back wall, above the desk, is a painting of* MARY PRESCOTT's *father, a distinguished-looking man, with twinkling eyes and a flower in his lapel. This portrait has its own light and switch. Around it are personal photographs of former crowned heads and international figures. Against the back wall on each side of the arch is a bookcase. Against the left wall above the bedroom door is a phonograph. Down-*

*stage left is a comfortable couch, a low coffee table in front of it, an end table at its left. Behind the couch is a table; a lamp is at its left end, a vase of flowers at the right end. There are chairs against the wall, down left and down right. In front of the bookcase, right of the arch is a bar-wagon with glasses, bottles of liquor, etc.*

AT RISE: MRS. MARY PRESCOTT, *a handsome, distinguished woman of young middle age, wearing heavy horn-rimmed glasses, is seated at her desk studying some manuscript pages, occasionally underscoring and punctuating. It is a speech she is to make that evening.*

KATHLEEN MURRAY, *her secretary, enters from the hall left, with a sheaf of letters. She comes to above the desk.*

MARY *finishes her work on speech, which she hands to* KATHLEEN.

#### MARY

All right, Kathleen. Here's my speech. Double-space it as usual. Underscore the words I've underscored and indicate those pauses I've marked in my copy.

#### KATHLEEN

Is it ready to be released?

#### MARY

Not yet. The new paragraph still has to be cleared from Washington. Have that on a separate page. I'll know about that when you meet me at the dinner.

(KATHLEEN *hands her the batch of letters.*)

4

KATHLEEN

These letters should be signed tonight, Mrs. Prescott. The others can wait until tomorrow.

(MARY *takes them and starts to glance through them and sign them.*)

MARY

I wish Washington would call. I have to be getting dressed.

KATHLEEN

You have that appointment with Elliott Clark.

MARY

Kathleen—don't you think you could take him off my hands?

KATHLEEN

Oh, no, Mrs. Prescott! This is much too important. Every time he's mentioned the Prescott Proposals on the air he's been so noncommittal.

MARY

Yes, I know. And people do listen to him. It would be nice to have him committal.

KATHLEEN

He said he only wanted five minutes. But I made the appointment here at the house so you could take your time and go to work on him. I didn't know about the cocktail party.

MARY

I didn't know about it either, until I heard myself inviting them.

KATHLEEN

You used to get along so well with Mr. Clark. If you could just get him on our side, Mrs. Prescott.

MARY

Well, I'll try. (*She has revised one letter*) This letter doesn't sound just right, Kathleen. I'm afraid you'll have to retype it before you leave.
> (*She hands the letter to* KATHLEEN, *and as she goes on signing,* EMMA *enters.* EMMA *is* MRS. PRESCOTT'S *elderly housekeeper.*)

EMMA

Have you finished with this, Mrs. Prescott?
> (*She indicates the tea tray.*)

MARY

Yes, Emma. (EMMA *takes the tray, goes to window and looks out*) I'm sorry you can't go yet, Emma. It just can't be helped.

6

**EMMA**

It's all right, Mrs. Prescott. My brother's found a place to park right in front of the house. He's perfectly comfortable. And I warned them I'd be late.

(EMMA *starts back toward the arch.*)

**MARY**

(*Looking at her watch*)

I can't possibly be dressed by seven o'clock. But you can leave as soon as the first guest arrives.

**EMMA**

Thank you, Mrs. Prescott.

**MARY**

Is everything ready for cocktails?

**EMMA**

Yes, ma'am. Everything but the liquor.

**MARY**

That's fairly important, Emma.

**EMMA**

I didn't know how many were coming or who.

7

MARY

There'll be three. Monsieur d'Arceau usually takes Dubonnet. He may want a Martini. Scotch of course for Sir Audley. I don't think Dr. Masoud drinks. He may join me in a Coca-Cola.

EMMA

Very well, ma'am. (*The telephone rings.* EMMA *picks up the receiver of one phone*) Mrs. Prescott's residence . . . (*It rings again.* EMMA *picks up the other phone*) Mrs. Prescott's residence . . . One minute please . . . (*To* MRS. PRESCOTT) It's Washington, ma'am.

MARY

Oh, good! (*She takes the phone.* EMMA *exits with the tea tray*) Yes—put him on, please. Hello . . . Oh, hello Arthur, this is Mary Prescott again. Have you found the Secretary yet? (*Disappointed*) Someone must know where he is. I want to make a change in my speech tonight and it has to be cleared. Arthur, when I was appointed to the United Nations it was you who briefed me on clearance, remember? You have me so frightened I've hardly been able to write to my mother . . . It went very well. The Committee on Freedom of Information and of the Press got started today. The first meeting's always just organization . . .

> (*The door buzzer has sounded and* KATHLEEN *has started for the door, stopping in the arch and calling off left.*)

8

KATHLEEN

I'll take it, Emma.
(*She exits right.*)


MARY

(*On telephone*)
Some of the committee are coming here for cocktails in about fifteen minutes. The British, the French, and Dr. Masoud, the Pakistani. No, not Petrovsky, but give me a week or two. Which reminds me—I must order some vodka. (KATHLEEN *and* ELLIOTT CLARK *appear in the arch.* ELLIOTT CLARK *is a handsome, middle-aged man of quiet charm and carrying the authority of his experience and present position. He has been a newspaper man and foreign correspondent and he is now our most distinguished and respected radio and television news commentator*) Come in, Mr. Clark. (*Into phone*) All right, Arthur. Please keep trying. It's important. (MARY *hangs up and rises*) It's nice seeing you again.


CLARK

It's been a long time.
(*They shake hands across the desk.*)


KATHLEEN

I'll redo this letter—and I'll watch your time, Mrs. Prescott.

(KATHLEEN *exits left.*)

MARY

Thank you, Kathleen. (*To* CLARK) You said you wanted five minutes. I'm afraid that's all the time we'll have.

CLARK

Well, that's two minutes more than we usually have. Every time I've maneuvered you into a corner at a cocktail party someone has come up and taken you away.

MARY

I know—and it's always been just as you were saying something I particularly wanted to hear.

CLARK

That's strange. My memory is that you were always saying something I particularly wanted to hear.

MARY

We'll have to listen to each other some time.

CLARK

I'm planning to listen to you Thursday night.

MARY

Thursday night? Where?

**CLARK**

On my broadcast. I'm hoping you will be my guest speaker.

**MARY**

Really?

**CLARK**

(*Sitting, left of desk*)
I'm devoting my entire program to the Prescott Proposals.

**MARY**

Oh? Do I speak before or after you've thrown cold water on them? As a woman, I would prefer to have the last word.

**CLARK**

I haven't meant to sound too doubtful about them. It's only natural for you to expect great things of them—they're your children.

**MARY**

They're not my children. They're the policy of the United States Government. I was very proud to be chosen to announce them, but I think it's unfortunate they've become known as the Prescott Proposals.

**CLARK**

Not at all. That's in their favor. And choosing a woman to sponsor them, and especially you, was a stroke of genius. It almost restored my faith in the State Department.

MARY

If I thought that speaking on your program would help you understand the Proposals . . .

CLARK

I usually find the speakers on my program very convincing. Let's consider it settled.

MARY

It's not that simple. I'd have to write it. I couldn't get to that before tomorrow, and the clearance wouldn't come through before the day after.

CLARK

That's time enough. And since I'm going to talk about the Proposals too, I ought to give you a chance to charm me into the proper attitude. Can you spare me any time . . .
(*The telephone rings.*)

MARY

Excuse me, please. (MARY *answers telephone*) Oh . . . Hello, Arthur . . . Well, if that's the way it has to be done, I can dictate it over the phone. (CLARK *rises.* MARY *speaks to him*) Sit down. This may interest you. (*Into phone again*) Arthur, was the editorial in the *News* called to the Secretary's attention? We're still being misunderstood or misrepresented. I want to include in my speech tonight this paragraph —a clarification in the simplest possible language. Is the stenographer on? This is it: "The criticism that the United Nations has been used largely as a public forum for voicing the differences between nations is a valid one." . . . Am I going too fast for you? . . . Good . . . "The purpose of these recent Proposals of my government was very simple: That the United Nations explore, in the temperate atmosphere of closed committee meetings, their areas of agreement, in the hope that these areas of agreement may be later extended. We believe that there will be evidence that the present areas of agreement are large enough to reassure all nations, including Russia, that the solution to world problems lies in negotiation rather than war." That's all. Have you got that? Arthur, as soon as the Secretary has seen this, get word back to me . . . Thanks, Arthur. (*She hangs up*) Well, Mr. Clark. Do you think that clarifies our position?

CLARK

Possibly.

MARY

You don't sound very clarified.

CLARK

As a realist, I have my doubts as to what will be accomplished.

MARY

Well—we've accomplished this much already. Russia has made it difficult to negotiate outside the United Nations.

Now we have her negotiating inside, which is even better.

CLARK

But will Russia ever really negotiate?

MARY

At least we have her talking—and listening. Under our Proposals, five committees already have been set up. The most important one, of course—the Committee on Disarmament.

CLARK

There's no area of agreement there.

MARY

But there is! Nations had already agreed not to use chemical warfare or germ warfare. In the last war, they kept that agreement. Can't we go on from there—step by step—perhaps even to atomic warfare—in our new hope that atomic energy can be turned to peaceful purposes? At least, can't we try? I'd like really to talk this over with you some time.

CLARK

We'll have to talk about the broadcast. Can you spare me any time tomorrow? Are you free for dinner?

MARY

Well, until I check at my office I'm not sure I can do the broadcast. I'll have my secretary call you tomorrow morning. I'd like to do it—even if you were the only one listening.

CLARK

I can assure you of that, at least. I'll hear from you in the morning, then. I can't thank you enough.

(*He rises.*)

MARY

Wait a minute. If I'm to be on your program, I assume that you would introduce me.

CLARK

Elaborately.

MARY

That worries me. I'm afraid I'd have to hear that before . . .

CLARK

Oh, I can tell you now. I've made some notes. (*He refers to a sheet of paper, which he takes from his pocket*) I'd begin with something about your father—a career diplomat—chargé d'affaires Paris, London, Berlin—Minister to Norway, Ambassador to Czechoslovakia.

MARY

I thought you were introducing me.

CLARK

This is what we call background. Describes your diplomatic education.

15

MARY

Yes. I know . . .

CLARK

When your father was recalled to Washington, just after the start of the last war, you were his hostess. Charmed Washington society in general and Senator Edward Prescott in particular. After your marriage to Senator Prescott, you were very important behind the scenes in Washington.

MARY

No one is important behind the scenes in Washington. Really, you commentators shouldn't believe everything you say.

CLARK

I'll substitute "witty and modest."

MARY

I'm not witty and I'm quite the opposite of modest.

CLARK

All right—witless and immodest.

MARY

Hadn't we better get on?

CLARK

When your husband died, you were appointed to fill out his term in the Senate. After your term expired, the President appointed you to the United Nations. I'll have it typed out and let you see it.

(KATHLEEN *has come into the arch.*)

#### KATHLEEN

I'm sorry, Mrs. Prescott. It's getting very late.

#### CLARK

I'll run along.

#### MARY

I have to dress. I'm making that speech tonight.

#### CLARK

Oh, yes—the World Forum dinner. Thanks for reminding me. I'll try to find room at the press table.

#### MARY

Oh, don't feel you have to be there . . .

#### CLARK

It's all right. I'll eat somewhere else first.

(*He smiles his good-bye and exits.* KATHLEEN *hands her the retyped letter and goes into the hall with* CLARK. MARY *reads the letter and* KATHLEEN *returns.*)

#### MARY

This is fine now, Kathleen.

(*She signs it and hands it back to her.*)

KATHLEEN

Did you win him over, Mrs. Prescott?

MARY

I forgot to try. Maybe I should have accepted his invitation to dinner. He's nicer than I remembered him. You'd better get started on that speech.

> (EMMA *enters with two bottles, one of Scotch and one of Dubonnet.*)

KATHLEEN

I can make it. I'll see you at the dinner.

> (KATHLEEN *exits, saying good night.* EMMA *puts a bottle of Scotch on the wagon.* MARY *notices the bottle.*)

MARY

Not that Scotch, Emma. The good Scotch. It's for the British Ambassador. (*She starts for the bedroom*) Whoever comes first, tell them I'm dressing. Ask them to help themselves to a drink and make themselves comfortable.

EMMA

Yes, ma'am.

MARY

Then you can run along. And have a good time.

> (*She goes into the bedroom and closes the door.* EMMA *takes the bottle of Scotch from the tray and*

*goes out. After a short pause the doorbell rings.* EMMA *returns with a decanter of Scotch, puts it on the bar-wagon and exits to answer door.)*

### EMMA
*(Offstage)*

Won't you come in, please? (JAN CAPEK—*pronounced "Chapek"—appears in the arch. He is a distinguished-look-ing, middle-aged Czechoslovakian. He comes into the room and* EMMA *follows him*) I'll take your hat. Mrs. Prescott was delayed. She's still dressing. She says to help yourself to a drink and make yourself comfortable.

### CAPEK

Thank you.
> (EMMA *exits right, with hat. Then we see her pass down the hall, exiting left.* CAPEK *stands surveying the room. It is evident he has never been here before. He notices the window curtains are not drawn and swiftly goes and closes them. We hear a knock on a door off-stage, left, then* EMMA's *voice.)*

### EMMA
*(Offstage)*

Mrs. Prescott.

### MARY
*(Offstage)*

Yes?

EMMA

May I run along now, Mrs. Prescott?

MARY

Come in a minute, Emma.

EMMA

I'm sorry about the Scotch, Mrs. Prescott. (*We hear a door close offstage. After a minute* EMMA *enters from the bedroom door, her hat and coat on*) Good night, ma'am.

MARY

Good night, Emma. Leave the door ajar.

EMMA

Yes, ma'am. (*To* CAPEK) Mrs. Prescott will be with you shortly. Good night, sir.
> (*She hurries out, right.*)

MARY

(*Offstage*)
Hello! Sorry I'm late. Be with you in a few minutes. Have you everything you want?
> (CAPEK *smiles and takes a little pause to consider his reply.*)

CAPEK

There is no cassis.
> (*There is a slight pause, then* MARY *speaks sharply.*)

20

MARY
*(Offstage)*

What did you say?

CAPEK

There is vermouth, but no cassis, Marushka. (MARY, *in negligee, sweeps into the room, stops and stares at* CAPEK) It has been so many years.

MARY

Jan! Why are you here?

CAPEK

I had to see you.

MARY

Did Petrovsky send you?

CAPEK
*(With smiling assurance)*

They do not know I am here.

MARY

Don't you realize the Russians are probably having you watched?

CAPEK

Yes—they are. But I have worked with them long enough in Czechoslovakia, and if you know their methods it's very simple. They are watching my hotel now.

MARY

Jan, I shall have to ask you to leave immediately.

CAPEK

Do not worry. After the Committee meeting, Petrovsky's personal physician put me to bed. I have been ill, Marushka, very ill.
(*His voice and eyes are hoping for sympathy.*)

MARY
(*Answering his statement only*)
Yes, I heard . . . when you arrived.

CAPEK

I'm still very ill.

MARY

I can't have you here, Jan. I must ask you to go.

CAPEK

Then where can I see you?

MARY

You'll see me at the Committee meetings, and only then. Come along, Jan.

CAPEK

Marushka!
(*She starts to show him to the door, then stops.*)

**MARY**

Wait a minute! Why were you appointed to that Committee?

**CAPEK**

Why not? I am a delegate to the United Nations.

**MARY**

But why *you?* Did the Russians ever know about us?

**CAPEK**

No one knows about us. They never will.

**MARY**

Jan—this is not only dangerous for you—it's dangerous for me.

**CAPEK**

I have been very careful. You are now a most important woman.

**MARY**

Jan—you must see you can't stay here.

**CAPEK**

Marushka, for fourteen years I learned to discipline myself.

**MARY**

Yes, I know about those fourteen years.

CAPEK

*(Pushing those years away with a gesture)*
I must talk about today. At the Committee meeting I saw
you for the first time since you left Prague. My discipline—
vanished. There was nothing but emotion . . . Marushka . . .

MARY

I looked at you today. I saw your face, but not you, Jan—
not the man I knew in Prague.

CAPEK

Yes, I could see what you thought of me. That's why I'm
here. That's why I have to talk to you—to explain myself.

MARY

It's no use, Jan. Once we meant a great deal to each other.
But that's been over for years. You had started on your way
—Hitler's way—before I left Prague.

CAPEK

I'm not here to explain why I worked with the Nazis or
why I became a Communist. I survived.

MARY

Yes—you survived.

CAPEK

But one thing is important to me. It may be that my life
has been a lie. But whatever I said to you when we knew

24

each other—whatever there was between us when I loved you—what I felt—was true. It is still true!

MARY

Are you ready to go now?

CAPEK

Marushka, I have so little to hold on to—that I want to keep. I can keep it only if you believe me! I can't go until you say you believe me!

MARY

My guests will be here any minute. They are men who know you. Jan—you must see you have to leave. (CAPEK *stands there struggling with himself, torn between his sense of danger and his emotions. Finally he exits. We hear the outside door close.* MARY *goes into her bedroom and shuts the door. After a moment,* CAPEK *reappears in the arch. He strides into* MARY's *bedroom, leaving the door open! Offstage:*) Jan!

JAN

(*Offstage*)

Marushka, I can't go until you tell me when I can see you again.

MARY

(*Offstage*)

Jan, if you persist in this, I shall have to resign from the Committee, and you know what that will mean.

*(Offstage)*

Marushka! Marushka!

*(The telephone rings. MARY enters the room. She speaks over her shoulder.)*

MARY

I warn you, Jan, if I have to do that, I will! (MARY *goes to the telephone*) Hello! Hello! This is Mrs. Prescott . . . Arthur, I didn't mean to sound angry. I'm terribly pressed for time. He liked it? Good, I'm glad he felt that way . . . (*She hears the heavy sound of something falling in the bedroom*) What did you say? Yes, it will be in the press release. Well, I've bothered you enough for one day, Arthur. I'm very grateful . . . Good-bye. (*She hangs up and hurries into the bedroom*) Jan! Jan! (*She comes swiftly into the living room to the bar, pours a glass of Scotch, and returns to the bedroom. In a moment, she comes back again, hurrying to the outside telephone and dialing a number. She is in a state of agitation*) Is the doctor there? When is he expected back? No. No. Thank you. Never mind. It doesn't matter. (*She hangs up. Then quickly dials again*) Long Distance? Will you get me Washington? REpublic 7–53 . . . (*The door buzzer sounds*) Never mind, Operator, cancel it . . .

*(She hangs up and moves away from the telephone. Her mind tries to form a plan. She starts for the arch. She stops, turns and starts toward the bedroom. She closes the bedroom door, and comes back to the middle of the room. The buzzer sounds again. She takes a second to compose herself and then exits through the arch. We hear voices offstage.)*

D'ARCEAU

*(Offstage)*

*Bonsoir, Madame. Comment allez-vous?*

SIR AUDLEY

*(Offstage)*

Hello! Are we too early?

(SIR AUDLEY MARRIOTT, *the British Ambassador to the United Nations, and* PAUL-EMILE D'ARCEAU, *a delegate from France, appear in the arch, dressed in dinner clothes, topcoats and homburgs.* MARY *follows them.*)

MARY

Now don't take off your things. You're not going to stay.

SIR AUDLEY

Why not?

MARY

The cocktail party's off.

SIR AUDLEY

Why?

MARY

I simply haven't time to be a hostess. I just got clearance on some changes in my speech. I have to go over it a couple of times. And it must be obvious to you that I'm not dressed.

D'ARCEAU

Mary, make your speech *en négligé.* Just looking at you I already believe every word you are going to say.

27

MARY

I'm serious! Run along. I'll be lucky to get there in time to make my speech. (*The doorbell rings*) That must be Dr. Masoud. (*She starts for the door*) Audley—you take him with you.

SIR AUDLEY

You have damn bad manners for a girl who was brought up in embassies.

MARY

That's why I have no respect for ambassadors.
(MARY *exits.*)

D'ARCEAU

You're practically one yourself, you know. Have you no self-respect?
(*The minute she is gone,* SIR AUDLEY *takes off his hat and coat and goes to the bar.*)

MARY

(*Offstage*)
How do you do, Dr. Masoud?

MASOUD

(*Offstage*)
Good evening, Mrs. Prescott.
(SIR AUDLEY *is pouring a drink, when she returns with* DR. ALI MASOUD, *the Ambassador from Pakistan to the United Nations.*)

**MARY**

Forgive my appearance. I don't usually receive guests like this. But you're not going to be guests. You're all going somewhere else for cocktails. (*She sees* SIR AUDLEY *with his drink*) Now, Audley, that's not cricket. Will you please, all of you—well, the simplest way to put it is: Get the hell out of here.

**SIR AUDLEY**

I was invited here for a drink and I need a drink. I have to listen to your speech tonight. You run along and make yourself alluring.
(*He goes to the sofa and sits.*)

**MARY**

Audley . . .

**SIR AUDLEY**
(*Holding up his Scotch*)
I'm just going to finish this.

**D'ARCEAU**

Then that gives me time for one.
(*He takes off his coat and goes to the bar and starts pouring his drink.*)

**MARY**

Dr. Masoud, I'm afraid I'm forced to offer you a drink—but just one.

MASOUD

Have you Pepsi-Cola?

MARY

I have Coca-Cola.
(*She goes to the bar and opens a bottle of Coca-Cola.*)

MASOUD

No ice.

D'ARCEAU

We are a bit early, Mary. Sir Audley insisted on driving his
Jaguar himself.

SIR AUDLEY

Must advertise home products.

MASOUD

There are rumors at the United Nations that Sir Audley
takes orders for them.

MARY

There *is* some Pepsi-Cola.
(*She opens the bottle of Pepsi-Cola.*)

D'ARCEAU

Red lights, speed limits, one-way streets mean nothing to
him.

##### SIR AUDLEY

A diplomat cannot be confined to one-way streets.
(MASOUD *has picked up his glass and* MARY *is pouring Pepsi-Cola into it. When the glass is half full he signals her to stop.*)

##### MASOUD

Now please, the Coca-Cola. (*A little bewildered she takes the Coca-Cola and fills up the glass*) America has taught me to like mixed drinks.

##### SIR AUDLEY

(*Moving toward bedroom*)
Come on, Mary. We don't need you. Get in here.
(*He reaches for the bedroom door.* MARY *drops the empty Coca-Cola bottle on the bar.*)

##### D'ARCEAU

Mary, you're not worried about your speech, are you?
(MARY *shakes her head.*)

##### SIR AUDLEY

I say, I believe we have upset you! I'm sorry. We'll finish our drinks and get out.

##### MARY

I'm sorry if I've been inhospitable. It's an important speech.

##### D'ARCEAU

We understand.

31

MARY

Then if you'll excuse me.

(*She goes to the bedroom door. She reaches for the knob but can't quite touch it. She stands there unable to go in.* SIR AUDLEY *has crossed to join the others.*)

D'ARCEAU

(*To* MASOUD)

I thought Petrovsky was in a very good mood at the meeting today.

SIR AUDLEY

Yes. Made me nervous. Jan Capek was very quiet. Don't know what that means—yet. (*He sees* MARY *at the door*) Mary, is anything wrong?

(*She turns and her face clearly reveals there is.*)

D'ARCEAU

Mary, what is it?

(*She stares at them blankly for a moment.*)

MARY

I have to throw myself on your friendship. I need help.

SIR AUDLEY

What can we do?

MARY

Jan Capek came to see me this evening.

D'ARCEAU

Capek?

SIR AUDLEY

Is he coming over to our side?

MARY

No, he came because—I knew him years ago in Prague. (*She indicates the bedroom*) He had a heart attack. He's dead! (*After a short pause of shock,* SIR AUDLEY *and* D'ARCEAU *go swiftly into the bedroom.* MASOUD *moves to the door, looking in.* MARY *moves to the couch and sits weakly.* SIR AUDLEY *and* D'ARCEAU *come out of the bedroom sober and concerned with their own thoughts*) I shouldn't have done this to you. I shouldn't have told you. Please go. Just forget you were ever here.

D'ARCEAU

We can't leave you with this—you need us.

SIR AUDLEY

Yes, Mary, this is damn serious. We shall have to think of something.

MARY

You mustn't be involved. I'll see it through. There's no other choice. Please go.

SIR AUDLEY

(*To* MASOUD)

I say, Masoud, I really think you should slip out. Paul-Emile and I are old friends of Mrs. Prescott's.

(MASOUD *moves slowly toward the arch*.)


MARY

Audley, I can't do this to friends.


SIR AUDLEY

Mary, there's more at stake than you realize. Capek's dying in your apartment . . .


D'ARCEAU

That could be a bombshell.


SIR AUDLEY

It would be a personal disaster—but more than that. It could do great damage to the Prescott Proposals.


D'ARCEAU

Just now—when there's a promise of working together.


SIR AUDLEY

They are making real progress on disarmament—there's some hope. (MASOUD *stops and gives his attention*. SIR AUDLEY *speaks to him*) D'Arceau and I will have to work something out. We can't let this happen. You go ahead—forget you were here.

34

# THE PRESCOTT PROPOSALS

### MASOUD

If I can be of any service—the United Nations is more important than any one of us. I don't understand. Why should the Proposals be in danger?

### D'ARCEAU

Mary, why did Capek come to see you?

### MARY

Before the war, when my father was Ambassador at Prague —we were in love with each other.

### SIR AUDLEY

*start*

Mary, you must recognize—with your present importance —and Capek a Communist—the newspapers—some newspapers at least—and all the unscrupulous politicians—would utterly destroy your position.

### MARY

Yes, I know. I'd have to resign.

### SIR AUDLEY

But, Mary—if you did have to resign, you know what that would do to the Proposals . . .

### MARY

I'll have to face that.

35

D'ARCEAU

We can't let you face that. We can't let ourselves face that. (*He rises and goes to* SIR AUDLEY) Audley, can't we—couldn't we...

(*He looks toward the bedroom.*)

SIR AUDLEY

Exactly! We have to! Now, here's our story: (*He thinks it out as he talks*) When we stopped for a red light at Second Avenue and 48th Street, remember? Capek was standing there—on the corner, looking lost—as a matter of fact, looking ill. You saw him first, you hailed him. I offered him a lift. He asked us to drop him at his hotel. We started for it—he had this—attack—the Czech headquarters was closer—and that's where we're going to take him.

MARY

You can't do this. I can't let you.

SIR AUDLEY

Mary, they'll take our word. They can't question us.

MARY

No! I can't!

D'ARCEAU

(*To* MASOUD)

It would be even better if you were with us.

36

MASOUD

My hotel doorman might remember. He had trouble finding me a taxi.

(SIR AUDLEY *gets into his hat and coat.* PAUL-EMILE *follows his example.*)


SIR AUDLEY

(*To* MASOUD)

All right. You go out on the pavement. My car's right in front of the house. When it's clear sailing—Mary, you have to stand at the window—(*To* MASOUD *again*) when it's clear sailing you glance at Mary—then disappear down the street —and Mary, you let us know.

(MARY *is at the bedroom door. She stands barring the way.*)


MARY

You can't do this!


SIR AUDLEY

Mary, no nonsense.


D'ARCEAU

We must do it.


MARY

No! I can't let you. (*The doorbell rings. The men look toward the door, then back at* MARY) I wasn't expecting anyone else.

37

### SIR AUDLEY

You'll have to answer it. Get rid of them.

(MARY *walks slowly toward the arch and out. The others move up within hearing distance. We hear a door open and then a man's voice.*)

### PETROVSKY
(*Offstage*)

How do you do, Mrs. Prescott?

(*Through the arch enters* ALEXIS PETROVSKY, *Russian Ambassador to the United Nations. He is a heavy-set man with a handsome but expressionless face. He is dressed in a business suit. He stops at the sight of the other men but quickly conceals his surprise at finding them there.*)

### SIR AUDLEY
(*Cordially*)

Hello, Petrovsky! (*He takes off his coat.* D'ARCEAU, *watching him, follows suit*) We're all very prompt, aren't we? Mrs. Prescott didn't tell us you were joining us for cocktails.

(MARY *has entered the arch.*)

### MARY

Mr. Petrovsky wasn't expected. Did you come to see me?

### PETROVSKY

It is a little strange to find our Committee meeting in my absence.

D'ARCEAU

But you're not absent.

SIR AUDLEY

And it's not a Committee meeting.

PETROVSKY

But the entire Committee is here.

D'ARCEAU

Entire Committee?

SIR AUDLEY

(*Looking around*)

I say, are we? Well, not quite.

PETROVSKY

(*Cutting in sharply*)

Where is—Capek?

D'ARCEAU

Capek?

PETROVSKY

He's here. In this house. He was followed here. Where is he?

(*There is a tense pause.* SIR AUDLEY *steps to the bed-room door and throws it open.*)

39

SIR AUDLEY

He's in this room! (PETROVSKY *starts for the bedroom*) He's dead.

> (PETROVSKY *stops, stares at him, then brushes past him into the bedroom.* MARY *goes to left of desk, braces herself against it.* PETROVSKY *comes out of the bedroom to in front of the sofa.*)

PETROVSKY

How did he die?

SIR AUDLEY

Heart attack . . . must have been.

PETROVSKY

Why should I believe that?

D'ARCEAU

Petrovsky! He had a heart attack on the boat. He had to be carried off.

SIR AUDLEY

You've had him in hospital almost ever since he landed.

> (PETROVSKY *is silent a moment, turns and looks at* MARY, *then goes to her. The chair left of desk is between them.*)

PETROVSKY

Did Capek come here for political asylum?

MARY

No, we knew each other years ago in Prague.

SIR AUDLEY

Look here, Petrovsky, this mustn't become public.

PETROVSKY

Why was he here? What kind of a deal was he trying to
make?

MARY

His coming here was entirely personal.
(PETROVSKY *pushes the chair aside and steps close to*
MARY.)

PETROVSKY

I want the truth.

D'ARCEAU

One minute, Petrovsky. You're in Mrs. Prescott's home.
She's not a Russian, or a Pole, or a Czech!

SIR AUDLEY

Quite right, d'Arceau.

PETROVSKY

Did it have anything to do with the Prescott Proposals?

41

D'ARCEAU

Petrovsky, they knew each other in Czechoslovakia.


MARY

Years ago we meant a great deal to each other.


PETROVSKY

(*Disbelievingly*)

Are you suggesting that he was your lover?


MARY

(*Defiantly*)

Yes, we had been lovers!


PETROVSKY

What you say could not be true. We would have known about it.


MARY

No one knew. We had to be sure no one knew. My father was Ambassador.


PETROVSKY

(*Relentlessly*)

He came here for a purpose. What did he want?


MARY

(*With spirit*)

He wanted a chance to explain himself—to justify himself. I told him to get out.

**PETROVSKY**

Yes? What was he doing in your bedroom?

**MARY**

He followed me there. I was called to the telephone. While I was talking I heard a fall. When I went back he was dead. (*She sinks into the chair* PETROVSKY *has moved.*)

**SIR AUDLEY**

Petrovsky, his dropping dead here makes things difficult for all of us. D'Arceau and I had a plan. We were going to put Capek in my car and take him to the Czech headquarters.

**D'ARCEAU**

Our story would be we saw him on a street corner looking ill. We gave him a lift. He had this attack in the car.

**PETROVSKY**

That would be your story, not mine.

**SIR AUDLEY**

Petrovsky, your government has said it's sincerely interested in the Prescott Proposals.

**D'ARCEAU**

If Capek is found here—if Mrs. Prescott has to tell her story . . .

SIR AUDLEY

That might well be the end of them. (PETROVSKY *is silent*)
We might just as well find out where we stand tonight—now.
(PETROVSKY *continues silent for a moment.*)

PETROVSKY

I do not believe her story.

(*He turns away. There is a moment of tension, then*
MASOUD *moves quietly down to a position beside* PE-
TROVSKY.)

MASOUD

(*Very quietly*)

Alexis, I do believe Mrs. Prescott's story. I was here when
she first told it. But if I read it in the newspapers I am not
sure I would believe it. I would think—as you did—that
Capek came here to sell out. The defection of another man of
Capek's importance would not be good for the Soviet Union
at this moment. I do not think you can afford it.

(*After a moment* PETROVSKY *moves slowly down right.
The men are watching him closely.* PETROVSKY *comes
to a decision, goes to the desk, sits, pulls the telephone
to in front of him and dials a number. As* PETROVSKY
*speaks,* SIR AUDLEY *quietly moves nearer to him and
listens carefully, obviously understanding what he is
saying in Russian.*)

PETROVSKY

(*Into phone, in Russian*)

Petrovsky . . . Get me Smirnoff . . . You are to place Serbitchenko in custody immediately. He is to be allowed to

speak to no one and no one must speak to him. You will arrange transportation for him to Moscow on the first available plane. None of your business! Let me talk to Serbitchenko.

(*As he waits,* SIR AUDLEY *turns and gives* D'ARCEAU *a reassuring gesture and smile.*)

#### MARY

I can't go through with this. I must call the State Department.

(SIR AUDLEY *places his hand reassuringly on* MARY'S *shoulder.*)

#### PETROVSKY

(*Into phone, still in Russian*)

Serbitchenko? Petrovsky . . . You have succeeded in making a fool of me. The man you were following was not Capek. You have placed me in a position that was embarrassing and humiliating. You have damaged the prestige of the Soviet Union. You are to be returned at once to Moscow under charges . . . How dare you argue with me? That is enough!

(*He hangs up sharply.*)

#### SIR AUDLEY

(*To* PETROVSKY)

Thank you, Petrovsky. But weren't you being a little hard on him? After all he did follow Capek here.

#### PETROVSKY

(*Smoothly*)

He made a fool of me. You heard me tell him that. Letting me come here and create a situation because he mistook someone else for Capek.

45

SIR AUDLEY

Yes, but to ship him back to Moscow under charges.

PETROVSKY

(*Rising*)

I will handle this in my own way—you are free to handle it in your own way.

(*He starts out.*)

SIR AUDLEY

One minute, Petrovsky. One part of this we must all handle in the same way. (PETROVSKY *stops in the arch*) Let's be sure we understand each other—all of us. Damn serious business, this, you know. We're all at each other's mercy. This is my personal word of honor—I swear that not one word of what has happened here tonight will pass my lips to anyone. I'm going to ask the same of all of you. D'Arceau? (*He holds out his hand to* D'ARCEAU. D'ARCEAU *comes over to* SIR AUDLEY *and gives him his hand*) Mary? (MARY *rises and gives him her hand*) Dr. Masoud? (MASOUD *moves silently to* SIR AUDLEY *and shakes hands*) Petrovsky? (*After a bare second's pause* PETROVSKY *comes down and gives* SIR AUDLEY *his hand. There is a tense moment of silence, then* PETROVSKY *disengages his hand, turns abruptly and goes out*) We have to move swiftly. (SIR AUDLEY *and* D'ARCEAU *get into their coats*) Masoud, you're to signal Mary. (MASOUD *exits into the hall*) Mary—the window.

(*He and* D'ARCEAU *go into the bedroom.* MASOUD *comes back with a hat.*)

MASOUD

This hat. Capek's.

> (*He goes into the bedroom, returns immediately without the hat and exits through the arch.* MARY *has moved slowly to the window, pulls a corner of the drapes aside and looks out. After a space of time, she turns and calls toward the hall.*)

MARY

Now, Sir Audley!

> (*A few seconds later we see* SIR AUDLEY *and* D'ARCEAU *passing through the hall with* CAPEK *between them. His arms are around their shoulders. It is almost as if he is walking with their support.* MARY *is standing looking out the window as the curtain falls.*)

*Curtain*

# ACT TWO

## ACT TWO

### SCENE 1

*A committee room at the United Nations. A single door up left leads to the staff room. A double door in the back wall, right, leads to the corridor.*

*Center there is a large curved committee table with seven chairs. On the desk in front of six of the chairs are the names of the countries represented on the Committee. Reading from stage right to left they are U.S.S.R., Czechoslovakia, United Kingdom, United States, France and Pakistan. There is no sign before the third chair from the right. There are other side chairs available for staff members, along the walls. A stenographer's table, a chair at each end, is in the well of the conference table.*

*The CONFERENCE OFFICER's desk is against the left wall downstage. On it is an intercom telephone. Instead of a bell, there is a light on this desk which flashes when the telephone rings.*

*Across the back wall is a large map of the world.*

AT RISE: DR. MASOUD *is seated in the end chair, stage left, of the committee table. He is studying a report. On the table in front of him are other reports, several American magazines and two or three books. He is in deep absorption.*

THE CONFERENCE OFFICER, MR. FERNANDEZ, *a young man, is distributing mimeographed papers, bound together, on the committee table in front of each chair. The* CONFERENCE OFFICER *answers telephone, which has flashed its light.*

CONFERENCE OFFICER

Hello? The Committee on Freedom of Information and of the Press. The Committee will meet in about fifteen minutes. (*He hangs up and exits, left.* KATHLEEN *enters.*)

KATHLEEN

Oh, Dr. Masoud.

MASOUD

Miss Murray.

KATHLEEN

I was looking for Mrs. Prescott.

MASOUD

I haven't seen her today. Is it anything urgent?

KATHLEEN

She didn't come to her office this morning. She didn't even call. That's not like her.

MASOUD

Can I help you find her?

52

KATHLEEN

No, never mind. I just felt a little uneasy. I'll look again in the lounge.

(ALAN DRAPER *enters. He is a young man on the staff of the United Nations Department of Information. He is followed by* ELLIOTT CLARK.)

DRAPER

Hello, Miss Murray.

KATHLEEN

(*Seeing* CLARK)

Good afternoon, Mr. Clark.

CLARK

Good afternoon. I was supposed to get word from Mrs. Prescott this morning about a broadcast.

KATHLEEN

Well, I haven't been in touch with her today myself. I'm trying to find her now. Why don't you wait here?

(KATHLEEN *exits.*)

DRAPER

Dr. Masoud, this is Mr. Clark—Elliott Clark. Dr. Masoud of Pakistan.

CLARK

Your Excellency.

DRAPER

Is it all right for Mr. Clark to wait here for Mrs. Prescott?

MASOUD

Certainly.

DRAPER

If you want me again, I'll be in my office.

CLARK

Thank you, Draper. (DRAPER *exits.* CLARK *studies the map of the world for a moment*) It's a pretty big world, Your Excellency.

MASOUD

Not in this building, Mr. Clark. It's all right here—under glass.

CLARK

(*He extends a cigarette to* MASOUD)
May I offer you one, Dr. Masoud?

MASOUD

No thank you. I do not smoke.

CLARK

If I'm not interrupting anything important—I've been planning to get in touch with you.

54

MASOUD

Yes?

CLARK

I was hoping I could make an appointment to talk to you.

MASOUD

Certainly. Any time. I have great respect for you, Mr. Clark. Your broadcasts are very intelligent—and very valuable. I listen to you as frequently as possible.

CLARK

Thank you. My broadcast this week is going to be on the Prescott Proposals. Could it be before then? I'd like very much to include a statement from you.

MASOUD

It will take some time before the position of my government is crystallized.

CLARK

But you voted to explore them.

MASOUD

Yes—to explore them. But explorers do not know what they have discovered until they get there.

CLARK

Oh, then you feel as I do. . . .

MASOUD

Not entirely. I'm hopeful. The Prescott Proposals may be very important. They may well be a step forward. But . . .

CLARK

But what?

MASOUD

It has taken us many thousands of years to move this little way along the road. Americans always expect to find the millennium just over the next hill.

CLARK

Well, let me be fair to the Americans. We're under considerable pressure. Some people think we move too fast. But there are others, you know, who get very cross with us if we don't start providing the world with leadership every morning right after breakfast.

MASOUD

Leadership in the sense of direction, yes, that we welcome. Your immediate resistance to aggression in Korea was inspiring. But to expect that the solutions can be quick and easy—as you do in Korea.

**CLARK**

That's an instance of what I mean. We thought Russia would win the world's unpopularity championship. It seems we're giving them quite a race.

**MASOUD**

That is not true! It is not the unpopularity that is increasing, it is the confusion.

**CLARK**

In our foreign policy?

**MASOUD**

No, it is the confusion in our minds—we who are outside your country. We can understand your fear of Russia as a nation. You must be armed and well prepared. We can understand why you must not have a Communist in your State Department, in your atomic plants, and that you would not want them as teachers in your schools. What we do not understand is your fear of the idea of Communism—that if your citizens discovered it on a library shelf, heard it from a pulpit, or even from a college professor, that it would be so attractive that democracy could not compete with it. Have your political leaders no faith in the idea of democracy?

**CLARK**

It's not quite that, Doctor.

**MASOUD**

It must be that. Or they have no faith in the intelligence of your people.

**57**

CLARK

I think you've missed a couple of my broadcasts. I'm not reprimanding you for that. A great many people miss all of them.

MASOUD

And what did I miss?

CLARK

There's a difference, Doctor, between Communism as an abstract idea and a conspiracy to overthrow our government . . .

MASOUD

Yes, but . . .

CLARK

I admit some Americans have allowed the fear of the real danger—and there is one—to become a fear of something there is no reason to fear.

MASOUD

But all this excitement?

CLARK

This excitement, Doctor, this—hysteria—is a phase. We've had it many times before; it runs in cycles. If you knew our history . . .

MASOUD

I have studied your history. But even so, to me this . . .

CLARK

Is—a puzzlement?

MASOUD

A puzzlement? Is that an American word?

CLARK

No, I was just quoting. Perhaps you haven't seen *The King and I* . . .
    (*The look in* MASOUD's *eyes stops him.*)

MASOUD

Oh, yes, I now recall. It was spoken by an ignorant Asiatic barbarian. (*He is obviously offended*) If you will excuse me.
    (*He indicates the report and returns to it as if* CLARK *were no longer in the room.*)

CLARK

I'm sorry. I didn't mean to offend you. I hope we can talk about this again some time.
    (MASOUD *doesn't answer.* KATHLEEN *enters.*)

KATHLEEN

I found her. She was in the Meditation Room.
    (MARY *enters.*)

59

MARY

I'm so sorry about this, Mr. Clark.

CLARK

It's quite all right. I had to be over here this afternoon anyway.

MARY

Dr. Masoud, have you met Mr. Clark?

CLARK

Yes, we've been talking. Very stimulating.

MASOUD

How are you today, Mrs. Prescott?

MARY

Quite all right. (*To* KATHLEEN) I'll be back at the office at five o'clock, Kathleen. But I don't want to see anyone today. Make it light for me this week.

KATHLEEN

There's Pittsburgh on Friday.

MARY

I'm not up to that.

KATHLEEN

I'll send them the "very distressed and disappointed" wire.

MARY

You're a great woman, Kathleen.

KATHLEEN

I'll wait for a while in the lounge in case you need me.
(KATHLEEN *exits*.)

MARY

(*To* CLARK)

Forgive me for not getting word to you, but things have piled up on me and I just can't do the broadcast.

CLARK

I have an idea about that. I covered the dinner last night and I thought what you had to say was approximately brilliant.

MARY

Certainly not the way I said it. I stammered so I was putt-putt-putting like a motorboat.

CLARK

Yes, you seemed a little nervous at the start—but I thought the last four or five minutes were very effective.

61

MARY

Did they effect you?

CLARK

I was quite impressed. That speech has already been cleared, it wasn't broadcast, but we picked it up on a tape recording. Why can't I use the last four or five minutes on my program?

MARY

Well, that would simplify things.

CLARK

I could play back the part I want to use any time you want to hear it.

MARY

I'm not sure I want to hear it.

CLARK

Your voice records beautifully.

MARY

To me I sound just like Mortimer Snerd.

CLARK

I promised I'd type out the introduction and show it to you.
(*He hands her a paper. She glances at it.*)

62

**MARY**

You know—all this has been published. I'd rather have more time for my speech. My father's career was distinguished, but do you have to go into Paris, London and Czechoslovakia?

**CLARK**

I could cut that way down. I put all that in perhaps because I was a great admirer of your father's.

**MARY**

You were?

**CLARK**

He was very wise—and yet so debonair. After I met him, I had an attack of being debonair that lasted almost two years.

**MARY**

Where did you meet him?

**CLARK**

In Paris. I interviewed him once, when I was young . . .

**MARY**

And impressionable.

CLARK

You know, I've suddenly become aware of the fact that I am still impressionable.

MARY

We must have dinner together! But I warn you, I don't take these Proposals lightly. I sincerely believe they may lead to the saving of Western Civilization.

MASOUD

Which civilization?

MARY

Oh, I'm sorry, Dr. Masoud. I know your civilization is much older than ours.
(DR. MASOUD *rises.*)

CLARK

Western Civilization is just a phrase, Your Excellency. I should think by this time you'd have become used to hearing it.

MASOUD

(*On his way to the door on the right*)
I'm used to hearing it, Mr. Clark, but I shall never become used to it. (*To* MARY) I shall be back in time for the meeting.
(MASOUD *exits.* MARY *takes off the jacket of her suit and drapes it on the back of her chair.*)

64

CLARK

You're not going to your office?

MARY

The Committee will be meeting shortly, and I'm certainly not going near my office.
(*She goes to the* CONFERENCE OFFICER's *desk.*)

CLARK

Too many pests?

MARY

Too many pests and too many newspaper men. Or am I being redundant?
(*She dials the operator.*)

CLARK

Well, you can't blame the reporters for wanting to talk about the Capek case. It's quite a story.

MARY

(*Into telephone*)
Operator, this is Mrs. Prescott. My secretary, Miss Murray, is somewhere in the lounge. Will you put her on, please?

CLARK

I knew Capek slightly years ago.

65

MARY

Oh?

CLARK

When I first hit Prague, he was Chief of the Press Department in the Foreign Office.

MARY

When was that?

CLARK

Thirty-eight. You were there then. You must have known Capek.

MARY

(*Casually*)

I think I knew everybody in Prague. What were you doing there?

CLARK

A.P. Capek had a great deal of charm. Didn't you think so?

MARY

I found all Czechs charming—in those days. (*Into telephone*) Kathleen, I'm going to stay here. No, there's nothing I need. See you at the office.

(*She hangs up.*)

CLARK

When you met Capek over here—did he remember you?

66

**MARY**

He was only at that one Committee meeting. I suppose he recalled me—but people under the Russian influence don't greet Americans as old friends—publicly.

**CLARK**

You didn't talk to him?

**MARY**

There wasn't much chance. May I ask you a question?

**CLARK**

About Capek?

**MARY**

No. About the Proposals. I heard your broadcast the night they were announced. I've heard you many times since. Why do you have to be so neutral?

**CLARK**

I'm not neutral. I'm hoping—but keeping my fingers crossed.

**MARY**

It seems to me your fingers have been crossed so long they're practically braided.
  (*She returns to her chair.*)

CLARK

I'm not sure you understand. I'm a reporter. If I became a special pleader, I'd lose all my value.

MARY

(*With some emotion*)

I heard you broadcast from London during the war. I'll never forget that one night when you stood on a rooftop during an air raid. It made me proud you were an American. I wanted to be standing there beside you. You can't claim you weren't taking sides then.

CLARK

War is different.

MARY

Why?

CLARK

Emotions are naked then.

MARY

It's the same conflict now—decency against indecency, humanity against inhumanity.

CLARK

Then it has to come to war.

68

MARY

In Heaven's name, why?

CLARK

Because you can't negotiate with the Russians. They're not open to reason.

MARY

At least let us prove we're reasonable. If the Russians are not, then the rest of the world will know they're not. There must be some chink in their armor. After all, they're human.

CLARK

That's the fallacy. They're not. They're no longer human.

MARY

I have to believe the human race is all human, or I couldn't go on living.

CLARK

(*Quietly*)

If I can be this personal, it's important for me that you do go on living.

MARY

How you think and feel is important to me, too . . . (*He looks at her*) . . . because it's important to America.

**CLARK**

I wasn't thinking about America.

**MARY**

If you thought more about America, you'd have more faith in humanity.

**CLARK**

Yes—until I thought about Russia.

**MARY**

Perhaps to be a good commentator you shouldn't think at all.

**CLARK**

Supposing we continue this debate over dinner?

**MARY**

Oh, you have the recording. That relieves you of your obligation.

**CLARK**

I was going to take you to dinner to talk about the Prescott Proposals. Remember?

**MARY**

Aren't you tired of hearing me talk about the Proposals?

CLARK

I'll make a deal with you. I'll take you to dinner not to talk about the Prescott Proposals.

MARY

That's the most unusual invitation I've had for weeks. It sounds very gay and attractive. I'd like to hear you talk without having to tune in. (CLARK *smiles*) I'm serious. I'd like to know what you really think.

CLARK

I say what I think on my program.

MARY

But then you're talking to twenty million people. I'd like to have you just talk to me.

CLARK

Shall I call for you at your house about seven?

MARY

Better make it eight.
(*A* RUSSIAN AIDE *opens the door on the right, holding a brief case.* PETROVSKY *enters, takes the brief case and goes to his chair. The* AIDE *exits.*)

PETROVSKY

Good day, Mrs. Prescott.

MARY

Mr. Petrovsky, do you know Elliott Clark?

CLARK

How do you do, Your Excellency?
(PETROVSKY *glances at* CLARK, *looks away and sits down.*)

MARY

You've probably heard Mr. Clark broadcast.

PETROVSKY

I never listen to him. But don't think I don't remember all he has said about the Soviet Union.

CLARK

(*To* MARY)
I'll be seeing you again . . . (*He glances toward* PETROVSKY *and back at her*) . . . I trust. (*The door opens and* SIR AUDLEY *and an* AIDE *carrying his brief case, come into the room, followed by* D'ARCEAU) How do you do, Sir Audley?

SIR AUDLEY

How do you do?
(*They shake hands.* D'ARCEAU, *carrying his own brief case, passes them on his way to the table.*)

CLARK

Monsieur d'Arceau.

72

D'ARCEAU

Hello there.

CLARK

Sir Audley, you had quite a session last night with reporters and radio men.

SIR AUDLEY

Yes, and I never want to talk to one of them again.
(*He turns his back on* CLARK *and goes to his chair.*)

D'ARCEAU
(*To* CLARK)
And we are not going on "Meet the Press."

MARY

Paul-Emile, don't confuse him. Mr. Clark doesn't know there are any other programs than his own.

CLARK

Well, you nations are united about me, at least.
(CLARK *exits.*)

SIR AUDLEY
(*To* AIDE)
Thank you, Herbert. (*The* AIDE *exits. To* MARY) I tried to get you on the telephone this morning.

73

**MARY**

I woke early and took a long walk.

**D'ARCEAU**

How are you, Mary?

**MARY**

I'm all right.

**SIR AUDLEY**

We brought it off rather well last night.

**D'ARCEAU**

It went just as planned. Audley was *magnifique*.

**SIR AUDLEY**

But the reporters questioned us for over an hour. It was very . . . (MIROSLAV BABICKA, *alternate delegate from Czechoslovakia enters, a* CZECH AIDE *holding the door open for him. He is a typical satellite diplomat.* SIR AUDLEY *rises and goes to shake hands with him. The* AIDE *exits*) Glad you're with us, Mr. Babicka. Mrs. Prescott, Monsieur d'Arceau, you both know Mr. Babicka of Czechoslovakia. (*They exchange nods.* SIR AUDLEY *indicates his chair. To* BABICKA) You're here.

(*The* CONFERENCE OFFICER *enters, goes to his desk.*)

**BABICKA**

You're in good health, Mr. Petrovsky?

PETROVSKY

*(Indifferently)*

Thank you.

> *(The* PRECIS-WRITER *enters. He sits at right end of stenographer's table.* MASOUD, *entering, speaks offstage.)*

MASOUD

Yes, gentlemen!

> (EXPERTS *and* ADVISORS *of each nationality represented enter and are seated.* SIR AUDLEY *raps with the gavel.)*

SIR AUDLEY

The second meeting of the Subcommittee on Freedom of Information and of the Press is called to order. I have here the credentials of Mr. Miroslav Babicka, Minister from Czechoslovakia, who has been designated by his government to take the place of Mr. Jan Capek.

MARY

We're very happy to have you here, Mr. Babicka.

BABICKA

Thank you.

SIR AUDLEY

In front of you, you will find a copy of the minutes of yesterday's meeting.

> *(He holds up his copy.)*

75

D'ARCEAU

I move they be approved.

SIR AUDLEY

All in favor?
(PETROVSKY *is reading the minutes.*)

PETROVSKY

One moment. (*He finishes reading them and holds up his pencil*) Approved.

SIR AUDLEY

Motion carried. (MARY *holds up her pencil. This is the customary United Nations procedure to get the attention of the Chairman of a small committee*) The representative of the United States.

MARY

Mr. Chairman, it has been the hope of my government that these Proposals—a part of which this Subcommittee has been appointed to consider—be discussed as informally as possible. We're really constituted more as a working group than as a committee. I therefore move that we dispense with the services of the experts and advisors and of the précis-writer, that is, until we have reached a point in our discussions where we feel we can formulate a draft.

76

#### D'ARCEAU

I quite agree. It has been my observation that when we see our words are being taken down we all make speeches.

#### MASOUD

I second the motion.

#### SIR AUDLEY

Any discussion?

#### PETROVSKY

I reserve the right at any time to have what I say made a matter of record.

#### SIR AUDLEY

That's understood. It goes for all of us. Since that's your pleasure, thank you, gentlemen.

>    (*He nods to the* PRECIS-WRITER *and the* EXPERTS *and* ADVISORS. *They leave.*)

#### MARY

I feel better already.

#### SIR AUDLEY

We can now talk among ourselves quite informally. Dr. Masoud, will you be so kind as to act as *rapporteur?* I have examined the suggestions submitted to me yesterday in writing as to the items which should be included on our agenda.

A list of them has been made—you will find it before you. (*He lifts his own and the others pick up theirs. After glancing at them,* PETROVSKY *raises his pencil*) The representative of the Soviet Union.

#### PETROVSKY

I cannot accept them in this order. The items submitted by my government . . .

#### SIR AUDLEY

Mr. Petrovsky, it's up to the Committee to put them in final order. It seems to me that that's the first business of this meeting. (BABICKA *raises his pencil*) The representative of Czechoslovakia.

#### BABICKA

Mr. Chairman, I have an item here I wish to be distributed. (*The* CONFERENCE OFFICER *goes to* BABICKA, *takes some papers from him and distributes them*) Mr. Chairman, last night in examining Mr. Capek's official papers and records I found that through some inadvertence he had neglected to submit an item for the agenda which is most important. It is the position of my government that this should be among the very first items on our agenda. You now have copies of its draft and our reasons for taking this position.

#### D'ARCEAU
*(After a glance)*
But this proposes a restriction on the freedom of the press.

### MARY

Yes, this is quite contrary to the spirit behind the forming of this Committee.

### SIR AUDLEY

Mr. Babicka, the essence of the Prescott Proposals is to explore areas of agreement. You are proposing an item on which there has been historic disagreement.

### BABICKA

It is my understanding that the Prescott Proposals had as their purpose the establishment of world peace. No government is more eager for world peace than the Republic of Czechoslovakia. In 1950 we enacted this law which made it a most serious criminal offense for a newspaper to publish anything that could be interpreted as the advocacy of war. Nothing would serve the purpose of peace more than that all countries should enact a similar law and that is why we demand that this item be on the agenda.

### MARY

Freedom of the press is written into the Constitution of the United States.

### D'ARCEAU

In France the press must be free to state the truth.

SIR AUDLEY

We're not here to establish restrictions on the freedom of the press. I'm sorry, Mr. Babicka, but I'm afraid I'll have to rule this out of order.

BABICKA

For a proposal of my government to be treated so casually would be very unfortunate.

PETROVSKY

Certainly a proposal from any government should receive study and consideration.

D'ARCEAU

I could study this, but my position would have to be the same.

BABICKA

You have not even finished reading it.

MASOUD

Mr. Chairman, I think it would be wise for us to consider this.

*(The telephone light flashes.)*

MARY

I agree with Dr. Masoud. Every proposal must be given thorough consideration. (*The* CONFERENCE OFFICER *answers the telephone inaudibly*) But in return I would like to ask Mr. Babicka to reconsider submitting this item. We're here to achieve a meeting of the minds—in the true spirit of the United Nations, I might say in a renewed spirit—I think it would be unfortunate to start off on this note.

(*The* CONFERENCE OFFICER *goes over to* SIR AUDLEY.)

CONFERENCE OFFICER

Mr. Chairman, the Assistant Secretary-General wants to know if you will see Mr. Draper.

SIR AUDLEY

Did he say what about?

CONFERENCE OFFICER

No. Mr. Draper is waiting. He wants to see the Committee as soon as possible.

SIR AUDLEY

If there's no objection, let him come in. (*He nods to the* CONFERENCE OFFICER, *who exits*) Anyone know what this is about?

D'ARCEAU

Mr. Babicka, you did not release this statement to the press?

BABICKA

But no!
(DRAPER *enters*.)

DRAPER

Mr. Chairman . . .

SIR AUDLEY

Yes, Draper?

DRAPER

Sir, the Assistant Secretary-General would like to see you as soon as possible. He wants to set up a press conference for your Committee after your adjournment today.

SIR AUDLEY

We're just getting organized. We're not ready to give out a statement.

DRAPER

It's not about the work of the Committee, sir. It's about Mr. Capek.

SIR AUDLEY

Good Lord, they held d'Arceau and me for an hour last night.

D'ARCEAU

And they got me again this morning.

82

DRAPER

But there's been a new development.

PETROVSKY

So?

MARY

What new development?

DRAPER

I don't know how seriously it should be taken. Nothing may come of it.

MARY

But what is it?

DRAPER

The City of New York is demanding the body of Mr. Capek. It insists on holding an autopsy.

PETROVSKY

An autopsy!

MARY

But why?

DRAPER

There's some local law.

83

PETROVSKY

This is an outrage! What right have they?

DRAPER

If a person dies suddenly, without a doctor in attendance, there must be an autopsy to determine the cause of death.

SIR AUDLEY

He died of a heart attack. He was subject to them.

DRAPER

They're taking a very legalistic attitude.
(PETROVSKY *and* BABICKA *talk in Russian.* BABICKA *storms out, shouting Russian, obviously denouncing America.*)

PETROVSKY

Mr. Babicka questions the jurisdiction of New York City. He has gone to consult his delegation. He wishes me to say that this could happen only in America.

SIR AUDLEY

Very well, Draper. I'll see the Assistant Secretary-General.
(DRAPER *exits.*)

D'ARCEAU

There was no indication last night they did not accept our word.

84

SIR AUDLEY

(*Rising*)

But here they are back asking questions. I'll have to ask you to excuse me. I'm going to take a stand against any press conference. I'd like to have some of the Committee with me.

MASOUD

(*Rising*)

I'll be glad to go.

SIR AUDLEY

Thank you. (*To* D'ARCEAU) You come too, Paul-Emile.

D'ARCEAU

Of course.

MARY

Do you want me with you?

SIR AUDLEY

No, Mary. You've been through enough. Mr. Petrovsky?

PETROVSKY

Someone should stay here with Mrs. Prescott.

SIR AUDLEY

The Committee is in recess until we return.
(SIR AUDLEY, D'ARCEAU *and* MASOUD *exit.*)

MARY

It was kind of you to stay with me, Mr. Petrovsky.

PETROVSKY

That was not why I did it. I wanted an opportunity to talk to you. I need some information.

MARY

What information?

PETROVSKY

Can you give me the name of anyone in Czechoslovakia who knew of your relationship with Jan Capek?

MARY

Why do you ask me that?

PETROVSKY

I have gone a long way to help you. I think you should help me.

MARY

How would that help you?

PETROVSKY

It would give me peace of mind.

MARY

Isn't my word enough?

PETROVSKY

No.

MARY

It was very difficult for me to tell you about myself and Jan. I certainly can't be expected to prove it.

PETROVSKY

I have made inquiries in Czechoslovakia.

MARY

You've what?

PETROVSKY

I have a report on Capek's personal life.
(*He consults a report which he has taken from his brief case.*)

MARY

We gave each other our word—and you've broken it.

PETROVSKY

I did not use your name.

MARY

I still question what you've done.

PETROVSKY

I have a list of all the women in Capek's personal life. Your name does not appear. I regret to inform you, however, it is a very long list.

MARY

It was charming of you to tell me that. But I still must protest and I demand to know your reasons.

PETROVSKY

I must satisfy myself you are telling the truth.

MARY

Isn't it enough that Jan came to my apartment?

PETROVSKY

He was not the kind of man to take such a risk. Capek did not fool us.

MARY

Aren't you being somewhat frank?

PETROVSKY

I can always deny having had this conversation.

MARY

Well, you can't be any franker than that.

PETROVSKY

This I must know . . . (*The* CONFERENCE OFFICER *enters.* PETROVSKY *changes his tone*) I cannot be sure I agree with you, Your Excellency, but I have not reached that item yet. (*They pretend to study their reports. The* CONFERENCE OFFICER *puts a sheet of paper before each delegate's chair, then exits. As soon as he leaves* PETROVSKY *speaks sharply*) Capek came to you to sell out. What were his terms? What did he offer? Tell me the truth.

MARY

(*Calmly*)

If you can't take my word—if what you believe is true— why didn't I say so? None of us would be in this horrible position.

PETROVSKY

That has occurred to you, eh, a little late?

MARY

What has occurred to me?

PETROVSKY

That you could have said Capek was there to betray Czechoslovakia.

MARY

But that was not why he was there.

PETROVSKY

But you could have said it. You missed a very big chance. That you did not think of it is the only thing that tempts me to believe your story. You could have done us great damage. And yet you did not take advantage of it.

MARY

It's very discouraging to find we think in such different terms.

PETROVSKY

But not at all. That is why I agreed to go along.

MARY

So it wasn't to help us go on working here together and . . .

PETROVSKY

Your government has not overlooked a chance to hurt us. This demand for an autopsy—this is not the City of New York —it is to keep alive suspicion of Czechoslovakia and the Soviet Union.

MARY

I regret what has happened as much as you do. It will just increase international tension. And I have a suggestion. I do

90

hope you'll consider it. (*The* CONFERENCE OFFICER *enters and sits at his desk. There is a moment's silence, then* MARY *speaks to the* CONFERENCE OFFICER) Mr. Fernandez, will you be good enough to get me copies of the records of the first five meetings of the 1952 Subcommittee on Freedom of the Press?

CONFERENCE OFFICER

Yes, Your Excellency. It may take a few minutes.

PETROVSKY

We can wait.
(*The* CONFERENCE OFFICER *exits.*)

MARY

Mr. Petrovsky, I agree with the position Czechoslovakia has taken. But why couldn't this happen? Why couldn't Czechoslovakia issue a statement maintaining its position that New York City has no jurisdiction over this, not yielding at all on principle, but in the interest of good international relations let them consent to the autopsy. It would get the story out of the newspapers and it would soon be forgotten. Let them hold the autopsy.
(*There is a pause.*)

PETROVSKY

Can you assure me Capek was not given poison?

MARY

Yes! I can! Can you give me the same assurance?


PETROVSKY

That's what I mean—the American attitude. Suspicion.


MARY

Mr. Petrovsky—it would clear the air.


PETROVSKY

(*Thoughtfully*)

Yes. The American newspapers must think they have Czechoslovakia by the throat and are enjoying it. It would be very good to get it out of the papers. (*After a pause of thought, he shakes his head*) But I cannot speak for the Czechoslovakian government.

(BABICKA *enters.*)


BABICKA

(*In Russian*)

We are taking a determined stand. We will not consent to the autopsy.


PETROVSKY

(*In Russian*)

Not so fast—I want to talk to you about this.

(PETROVSKY *and* BABICKA *talk quietly in Russian as* SIR AUDLEY, D'ARCEAU *and* MASOUD *enter.*)

SIR AUDLEY

I'm afraid we will have to hold a press conference after all.

MARY

Must we?

SIR AUDLEY

Well, I tried to argue against it; but the Assistant Secretary-General pointed out that inasmuch as this Committee deals with the freedom of the press it would be unwise to refuse to see newspapermen.

(CONFERENCE OFFICER *enters with reports, which he hands to* MARY.)

CONFERENCE OFFICER

Mrs. Prescott, these are the reports you asked for.

MARY

Thank you.

(*For a moment the voices of* PETROVSKY *and* BABICKA, *speaking Russian, are raised, the conversation ending with a peremptory order from* PETROVSKY.)

SIR AUDLEY

(*Sitting*)

Let's get back to business. Let's see—where were we?

93

MASOUD

We had before us the Czechoslovakian proposal.

SIR AUDLEY

Well, as it seems to be the feeling of the Committee, I am prepared to accept it for consideration. But since it is the last item submitted it will have to take its place as the last item on the list.

BABICKA

I accept that, Mr. Chairman.
(D'ARCEAU *holds up his pencil.*)

D'ARCEAU

Mr. Chairman, I think our time will be wasted. If we are to be faced with proposals that are obviously conceived to create dissension among us . . . (BABICKA *holds up his pencil*) . . . there is little hope that this committee will have any success whatsoever.

BABICKA

Mr. Chairman.

D'ARCEAU

Furthermore . . .

SIR AUDLEY

(*To* D'ARCEAU)

Will you yield? (*To* BABICKA) The representative of Czechoslovakia.

94

### BABICKA

Mr. Chairman, a motive has been attributed to Czechoslovakia which I must reject. My government is entirely willing to co-operate toward peaceful solutions. May I say something not pertinent to our discussions, but reflecting my government's attitude? In the matter of the demand for an autopsy on the body of Mr. Jan Capek—you know my government's position in this. We are determined to maintain this position. (MARY *and* D'ARCEAU *raise their pencils*) However . . .

### SIR AUDLEY

Please go on.

### BABICKA

My government is prepared to issue a statement reasserting its position that the City of New York is without jurisdiction, but, in the interest of international comity, waiving its objection and granting permission for the autopsy.

(*The others indicate their relief and pleasure.* PETROVSKY *raises his pencil.*)

### PETROVSKY

Mr. Chairman.

### SIR AUDLEY

The representative of the Soviet Union.

THE PRESCOTT PROPOSALS

PETROVSKY

The news of the magnanimous action of the government of Czechoslovakia comes to me with great pleasure. I hope in our future discussions we will all remember the co-operation of a government of Eastern Europe.

SIR AUDLEY

The Secretary-General doesn't know about this.

BABICKA

There has not yet been time.

MARY

Mr. Chairman, this is a matter of immediate importance.

SIR AUDLEY

I was about to suggest that. (*To* CONFERENCE OFFICER) Mr. Fernandez, would you see if Mr. Hammarskjold is free to see the representative of Czechoslovakia? Mr. Hammarskjold was with us upstairs. He is very concerned about this. (*The* CONFERENCE OFFICER *dials the telephone.* BABICKA *watches* PETROVSKY *for a cue*) I'm sure we would all be willing to take a short recess while Mr. Babicka reports this decision to the Secretary-General. (BABICKA *rises and closes his brief case. There is a murmur of assent from* MARY, D'ARCEAU *and* MASOUD) Is there any objection?

(*The* CONFERENCE OFFICER *is speaking on the phone.*)

PETROVSKY

No recess is necessary.
(BABICKA *sits down.*)

BABICKA

I would not wish to interrupt the work of this Committee.

PETROVSKY

During Mr. Babicka's absence we can proceed.

BABICKA

Yes.
(BABICKA *rises again.*)

PETROVSKY

Any conclusions we reach among us can be reviewed after
Mr. Babicka returns.

CONFERENCE OFFICER
(*Hanging up the phone*)
The Secretary-General is free to see Mr. Babicka.

BABICKA

If you will excuse me.
(BABICKA *hurries out.*)

97

PETROVSKY

It will be a great relief to stop the insinnuendoes of the American press.

MASOUD

Mr. Chairman—can we not now with a new serenity consider the difficult question of the agenda?

SIR AUDLEY

You have each the list of the items suggested.
(MARY *holds up her pencil.* SIR AUDLEY *nods to her.*)

MARY

Mr. Chairman, I move that items one, two and three be accepted in their present order.

MASOUD

I second the motion.

SIR AUDLEY

Any discussion?

MASOUD

The distinguished representative of the United States obviously questions, as I do, the position of the fourth item. I think that the question of the legal responsibility of the individual journalist is a doubtful part of our discussions.

98

# THE PRESCOTT PROPOSALS

### D'ARCEAU

I move the question.

### SIR AUDLEY

The motion is to accept the first three items of the agenda in their present order. All in favor? (*All but* PETROVSKY *raise their pencils*) Opposed? Mr. Petrovsky, are you abstaining?

(PETROVSKY *raises his pencil.*)

### PETROVSKY

In favor.

### SIR AUDLEY

Carried unanimously, if it later meets with the approval of Mr. Babicka. Am I to assume that item five now becomes item four? (PETROVSKY *raises his pencil*) The representative of the Soviet Union.

### PETROVSKY

I move that item twenty-seven be placed as item four upon the agenda.

(*They all pick up their lists and find item twenty-seven.* D'ARCEAU *is the first to raise his pencil.*)

### SIR AUDLEY

The representative of France.

### D'ARCEAU

I regret I must object to the suggestion of Mr. Petrovsky. I would prefer to see item twenty-seven dropped altogether.

SIR AUDLEY

I think I should explain to Mr. Petrovsky, since this item was submitted by his government, that I gave it its deferred position deliberately. It will be extremely controversial.

PETROVSKY

I assure you it is one we must eventually face.
(MARY *raises her pencil.*)

SIR AUDLEY

The representative of the United States.

MARY

Mr. Chairman, may I address myself to the representative of the Soviet Union? (SIR AUDLEY *nods*) Mr. Petrovsky, the spirit of today's meeting has been so harmonious, since this meeting was called to order such progress has been made. I know that in the meetings which lie ahead there will be sharp differences between us. I think the longer the subjects which will provoke those differences can be postponed—the longer we can proceed in the present friendly and agreeable atmosphere . . .

PETROVSKY

I withdraw my motion. I find it impossible to resist the persuasion of the distinguished and amiable representative of the United States.

(*During the above the telephone light has flashed and the* CONFERENCE OFFICER *has answered it. He hangs up.*)

SIR AUDLEY

Splendid! We're forging ahead.


D'ARCEAU

I move that item five be regarded as item four.


PETROVSKY

I second the motion . . .
> (*The* CONFERENCE OFFICER *comes over and whispers to* PETROVSKY.)


SIR AUDLEY

Any discussion? All in favor? (*They all raise their pencils*) Carried unanimously.


PETROVSKY

If you will pardon me, Mr. Chairman. I am wanted on the telephone.
> (*He goes to the telephone. The* CONFERENCE OFFICER *exits.*)


SIR AUDLEY

Certainly. When Mr. Petrovsky is free we will come to the consideration of item six.
> (PETROVSKY *talks on the telephone in Russian, then switches to the Uzbec dialect.* MARY *turns to speak to* SIR AUDLEY. *He signals her to be quiet as he tries to listen.* MASOUD *abandons the agenda to return to the reading of one of the reports.* PETROVSKY *hangs up.*)

PETROVSKY

Mr. Chairman, I must be excused for a minute. I have received very disturbing news. My secretary is waiting for me in the corridor. I shall be back immediately.

(PETROVSKY *locks his brief case and exits.*)

D'ARCEAU

What was that all about?

SIR AUDLEY

I couldn't follow what he was saying. He started in Russian—some talk about the newspapers—then switched to some dialect—one of the Turkestani dialects, I think. We'll have to wait for him to come back. (CONFERENCE OFFICER *enters and sits at his desk.* SIR AUDLEY *notices* DR. MASOUD, *who is deep in a report*) I say, Dr. Masoud, you don't actually read all those reports do you?

D'ARCEAU

He reads everything. On that trip to San Francisco he read the whole railroad ticket.

(PETROVSKY *returns with a newspaper in his hand.*)

PETROVSKY

Mr. Chairman. This is most serious. I demand an executive session.

SIR AUDLEY

May we know the reason for this request?

PETROVSKY

When we are alone. Until then, I cannot even discuss it.

SIR AUDLEY

Any objections? (*To the* CONFERENCE OFFICER) Thank you, Mr. Fernandez.
(*The* CONFERENCE OFFICER *exits.*)

PETROVSKY

(*Holding up the paper*)

This is a vicious attack upon the Soviet Union, upon Czechoslovakia, upon the Communist world: vicious, diabolical, criminal, evil-minded, shameless! Someone—someone in this room, is guilty of a deliberate and treacherous maneuver to stir up hatred against my country!

D'ARCEAU

(*Rises*)

Petrovsky!

SIR AUDLEY

(*Rapping*)

I shall have to ask you to restrain . . .

**PETROVSKY**

This was done for one purpose—to incite suspicion and to bring discredit upon the Soviet Union.

**SIR AUDLEY**

You've made a very serious charge and I'd like to know the basis of it.

**PETROVSKY**

Very well! I will read you what I have just read! (*Reading from paper*) "Informed sources revealed today the reason New York City has pressed for an autopsy on the body of Jan Capek, Czechoslovakian delegate to the United Nations, who died suddenly last night. An anonymous telephone call to the District Attorney's office declared that he had not died as reported but met death in the apartment of a person highly placed in the United Nations . . ."

**MARY**
(*Rising and going to him*)

Oh, no! No!

**PETROVSKY**

". . . There are rumors that Capek had gone to this apartment to arrange for political asylum, and that this had been discovered by the Russians. Whether or not Capek met death by foul play may be determined by the autopsy." (MARY *takes the newspaper from him. The others are too stunned to speak*) Someone—someone in this room—has broken his word. I do not absolve any one of you! (*They all continue to stare at* PETROVSKY, *except* MASOUD, *who has turned away*) Not even you, Dr. Masoud! (PETROVSKY *looks at* D'ARCEAU) French politicians have always been able to use scandal.

### D'ARCEAU
(*In French*)
Petrovsky! You are talking like a madman!

### PETROVSKY
(*To* MARY)
Madame, a woman of your type would not hesitate to sacrifice herself to gain advantage for her country.

### SIR AUDLEY
(*Rising*)
Petrovsky! You've said enough!

### PETROVSKY
And the British know only too well how to exploit hatreds!

### SIR AUDLEY
I shall not dignify that by any comment.

### PETROVSKY
One of you has broken faith. Which one?
(D'ARCEAU, SIR AUDLEY *and* MARY *look away from one another, searching their minds. Then* D'ARCEAU *and*

MARY *look toward* SIR AUDLEY, *who is looking at* MA-SOUD. MARY *and* D'ARCEAU *look at* MASOUD, *who feels their eyes on him.* MASOUD *shifts uneasily in his chair.*)

**Curtain**

## Scene II

scene: mary's *apartment.*

time: *Late the same evening.*

*A small table radio is on the upper end of the desk. A telephone bell is ringing. After a pause* emma *enters and picks up the outside phone.*

#### EMMA
*(Into phone)*

Mrs. Prescott's residence. (*The telephone continues to ring. She puts down this receiver and lifts the other*) Mrs. Prescott's residence. No, Sir Audley, Mrs. Prescott isn't in yet. She didn't say, but I know it was a dinner engagement... I'll leave a note you called ... Yes ... Cheerio to you. (emma *hangs up, makes a note on a pad and exits. No sooner is she out of the room than the telephone rings again.* emma *returns, picks up the outside telephone*) Mrs. Prescott's residence. (*She is pleased to find she has picked up the right phone*) Mrs. Prescott is not at home ... I couldn't say ... Would you care to leave your name? ... What was that? ... Yes. (*She writes a name on the pad*) And the number? (*She writes this down*) I can't be sure, but I'll leave this note ... Very well.

> *(She hangs up and exits. After a pause we hear the outside door being unlocked.* mary *comes into the*

*arch and stands looking back toward the door. She is*
*wearing an evening gown and wrap and is carrying an*
*evening bag. After a pause we hear* CLARK *offstage.)*

CLARK

*(Offstage)*

Mary . . . Mary . . .

MARY

Yes.
(CLARK, *in dinner clothes, joins her in the archway. He*
*has a ten-dollar bill in his hand.*)

CLARK

Could I borrow a dollar? The taxi driver can't change a
ten-dollar bill.

MARY

I've heard of this racket.
(*She gives him a dollar bill.*)

CLARK

I save quite a bit of money this way. I owe you a dollar.
(*He starts out.*)

MARY

Just a minute. Not this time. (*She takes his ten-dollar bill*)
Now I owe you nine dollars. (*He exits.* MARY *goes to the*
*phone and dials a number. Into phone*) This is Mrs. Prescott
speaking. Is Sir Audley there? When is he expected home?
. . . Just tell him I called.

**EMMA**

*(Offstage)*

Is that you, Mrs. Prescott?

(EMMA *enters.*)

**MARY**

Yes, I'm home, Emma.

**EMMA**

Sir Audley called twice.

**MARY**

I just tried to reach him. Any message?

**EMMA**

No, ma'am. He said he'd call later.

(MARY *puts on her glasses and consults the desk pad.*)

**MARY**

Emma, what's this last number?

(CLARK *appears in the archway.*)

**EMMA**

Lackawanna 4–1000.

**CLARK**

Oh? The New York *Times.*

MARY

Emma, this is Mr. Clark.

EMMA

I recognized his voice right off.

CLARK

(*To* MARY)
You see—I have a following!

MARY

Emma, we'll both have a highball.

EMMA

Yes, ma'am, right away.
(EMMA *goes into the arch, then looks back toward* MARY *inquiringly.*)

MARY

The good Scotch.

EMMA

That's nice.
(EMMA *exits.*)

CLARK

You know, I can see you better without those glasses.

110

MARY

I always wear glasses in my office—and this happens to be my office.

CLARK

Well, come out of the office. (MARY *smiles, takes off her glasses and puts them on her desk*) And may I suggest that whenever you have your picture taken you leave them off.
(*She starts for her bedroom.*)

MARY

I have to do something to make me look intelligent. The glasses are my official uniform.
(*He stops her and takes her fur wrap off her shoulder.*)

CLARK

I prefer you in mufti—off-the-shoulder mufti.

MARY

The radio is on the desk.

CLARK

I'll get the news.

MARY

I'll be back in a minute.
(MARY *exits into the bedroom.* CLARK *strolls about the room happily. As he passes the bookcase, he glances at the titles. Then he goes to the desk and turns on the*

*radio. The voice on the radio, a news broadcaster, reads a current news item.* CLARK *starts for the bedroom.)*

#### CLARK

Mary!

#### RADIO VOICE

"Mrs. Mary Prescott today became the central figure in the Capek case." (CLARK *stops*) "The report of the toxicologist will be announced some time tomorrow. If poison is found, the District Attorney plans a Grand Jury investigation. Because of diplomatic immunity, the only member of Mr. Capek's Committee whom he could subpoena would be the American delegate, Mrs. Prescott. It is rumored that she already has been in touch with the District Attorney's office . . . (*The voice reads another current item, then*) The weather today . . ."

(MARY *has entered.* CLARK *turns off the radio.*)

#### CLARK

My timing was bad. I tuned in a little late. I tried to call you.

#### MARY

Any news?

#### CLARK

Oh, something about . . . (*He summarizes the first news item*) There was a mention of the Capek case.

MARY

Yes?

CLARK

The toxicologist's report is expected some time tomorrow.
(EMMA *enters with a tray.*)

EMMA

Well, here we are. Shall I make you each a highball?

CLARK

No, thank you, Emma. I'll take care of that.

EMMA

Is there anything else, Mrs. Prescott?

MARY

No, thank you, Emma. Good night.

EMMA

I'll take even more pleasure listening to you now, Mr. Clark.

CLARK

Thank you, Emma. Good night.
(EMMA *exits.* CLARK *starts to mix the drinks.*)

MARY

Well, as you were saying when you were so rudely interrupted . . .

CLARK

When?

MARY

At dinner. When I suggested we come home and hear the news. You had left Karachi for Calcutta on your way to Rangoon.

CLARK

You're not going to get any more of that free. You'll have to buy my book. It will be out in another month.

MARY

Oh, I won't buy it. They are always after me to review something.

CLARK

That's even better. You'll have to read it. (*He hands* MARY *a drink*) Here you are—with plain water.

MARY

You remembered . . .

CLARK

Yes.

(*There is a moment's pause.*)

MARY

Elliott, tell me, when you were in Pakistan did you meet Dr. Masoud?

CLARK

No, that year he was in the Pakistan Embassy in Moscow.

MARY

Oh, yes.

CLARK

Why? What about him?

MARY

Nothing. I find him a very interesting person—fascinating, in a way, but I can't always follow his mind. Sometimes his motives seem—obscure.

CLARK

Well, he's from the East. They don't arrive at conclusions by following the paths we're trained to follow. Sometimes, I know, they seem . . .

MARY

I believe the word is inscrutable.

CLARK

Yes—but don't worry about Dr. Masoud's integrity. Newspapermen trust him. That's always a pretty good sign.
(*The outside telephone rings.*)

**MARY**

That can't be important or it would be on the other phone
—my private number. I'm not going to answer it.
 (*It rings again.*)

**CLARK**

Can't you take the receiver off the hook?

**MARY**

Then they'd know I'm home.
 (*It rings again.* CLARK *picks up his glass and goes over
to the tray and mixes himself another highball. The
phone goes on ringing.*)

**CLARK**

It's driving me to drink. (*It rings again*) I don't see how you
can just sit there.

**MARY**

I'm being inscrutable by telephone.

**CLARK**

I can't stand not answering a telephone. I always figure it
may be some uncle of mine who's died and left me a million
dollars. And I haven't even got an uncle.
 (*The phone goes on ringing.*)

MARY

Well, I have. A rich one, too. You've finally driven me to it.
(*She goes to the phone, lifts the receiver*) Hello? . . . Hello? . . .
Uncle Theodore hung up.
>(*She hangs up and stands at the telephone with some-
>thing obviously on her mind.*)

CLARK

What's on your mind?

MARY

What?

CLARK

I've noticed several times tonight there's something bother-
ing you.
>(MARY *attempts a gay evasion.*)

MARY

As a matter of fact, I was thinking of you. This new side
of you, this optimism.

CLARK

What optimism?

MARY

Expecting a nonexistent uncle to leave you a nonexistent
fortune. Completely out of character.

117

CLARK

That's not what you were thinking.

MARY

It was related to that—something you said yesterday and again at dinner—there was no optimism then.

CLARK

What was it?

MARY

About Communism having dehumanized the Russians.

CLARK

Well, it has.

MARY

I can only say again that I don't believe any system can dehumanize 200,000,000 human beings.

CLARK

Yes—I recall. There was a glow about you at that particular moment. I can't remember the words you used, but I can remember wanting to be convinced, wanting to believe you. So I changed the subject, remember?

MARY

Yes. Why?

118

CLARK

I was losing my professional perspective. My emotions were being engaged.

MARY

Perhaps that's my cue to change the subject.

CLARK

Well, I'll yield this much—I'll reduce it from 200,000,000 to 7,000,000.

MARY

Is that because you know a woman can't resist a bargain?

CLARK

Let me say the Communist party members in Russia are dehumanized.

MARY

Dehumanized is a pretty strong word.

CLARK

You think so. Take the purge trials. Some of them sent their closest comrades, their dearest friends to death. In cold blood. After that you can never let your blood get warm again. You couldn't be human. You couldn't live with yourself.

MARY

There must be something human left.

CLARK

Don't ever count on it.

MARY

This afternoon I had a few minutes alone with Petrovsky. He was everything you say—cold-blooded and unfeeling. I almost lost heart. Then later, I made an appeal to him for co-operation and he couldn't have been more charming or amenable.

CLARK

Oh, he was?

MARY

Yes. I had a feeling that perhaps we could work together.

CLARK

Let me tell you about Petrovsky. (MARY *sits down*) Of all the Russians—don't trust Petrovsky! Does the name Nina Simonova mean anything to you?

MARY

Nina Simonova? It rings a faint bell. I can't tell you why.

**CLARK**

Her story didn't get much of a play over here. There was too much going on at the time. (*He pauses*) Nina Simonova was a Russian poetess. She was damn good—not epics—she had a lyrical gift for simple emotions. She and Petrovsky were in love with each other, very much in love. She wrote a poem about her love for her lover—no names mentioned—it could have been any woman in love. It became tremendously popular with the Russians almost overnight. But she had made a mistake. She made it very clear in her poem that her love for a man was the most important thing in her life. Nothing in the world was important to her except that love. Then it occurred to someone in Moscow that that was deviationist. Her love for a man was more important than her love for the state. She was denounced and sent to her death. The person to whom this occurred—the person who denounced her—was her lover, Petrovsky.

**MARY**

Oh no! To protect himself?

**CLARK**

And to protect the party. Don't trust Petrovsky! He can't afford to be human! He could never let himself have one human emotion—he could never face the memory of Nina Simonova!

(MARY *gets up and walks away from him.*)

**MARY**

I don't question the truth of what you've told me, but my mind simply rejects it.

CLARK

If you're going to try to negotiate with these people, you'd better know with whom you're dealing.

MARY

I have to keep my faith in humanity.

CLARK

Look—we've wasted a lot of time tonight differing with each other. Let's see whether the Prescott Proposals really work. Let's explore our areas of agreement.

MARY

Good! I'd like to! But can you think of any?
(*He goes to the bookcase and glances at a group of books.*)

CLARK

Don't you agree that the best passage he ever wrote was the scene between Lady Lufton and the Duke at the top of the staircase at Miss Dunstable's?

MARY

(*Excited*)
Trollope! You know Trollope!

122

CLARK

I could draw you a map of Barsetshire blindfolded. Which is your favorite?

(*She joins him at the bookcase.*)

MARY

Oh, at least half a dozen of them. *Doctor Thorne*, and *The Way We Live Now* and *The Eustace Diamonds*.

CLARK

You can't leave out *Barchester Towers* or *The Small House at Allington*. You haven't got *The American Senator*.

MARY

No, but I've read it. And that reminds me. I was reading his autobiography again the other night.

(*She takes a book from the bookcase, goes to the desk and gets her glasses.*)

CLARK

He may not be the world's greatest novelist, but I can read him when I can't read anyone else.

(*She goes to the couch and sits.*)

MARY

It took Trollope to tell me where I stood politically. Listen to this: "The conscientious Conservative thinks that the preservation of the welfare of the world depends on what he considers a divine inequality. The equally conscientious Liberal regards a continual diminution of this inequality as a series of steps toward a human millennium. What is really in the Liberal's mind is—I will not say equality, for the word presents to the imagination of men ideas of communism and insane democracy but a tendency toward equality."

CLARK

He wrote that seventy-five years ago!

MARY

"I think I am guilty of no absurdity in calling myself an advanced Conservative-Liberal." That's me! (*She removes her glasses and puts them on the end table*) I should have known you read Trollope!

CLARK

That's the nicest thing you ever said to me. Where did you run into him?

MARY

You can't be brought up in Philadelphia without knowing Trollope.

CLARK

That's right. Your father came from Philadelphia.

124

MARY

Came from and carried it around the world with him. He introduced pepperpot and scrapple into every capital of Europe.

CLARK

Scrapple! I love scrapple! Haven't tasted it in years. How did your father get it in Europe?

MARY

Emma. She makes the best scrapple this side of Chestnut Street. There's always some in the icebox.

CLARK

Can I stay for breakfast?

MARY

Can you eat breakfast now?

CLARK

I can eat scrapple now.

MARY

I'll tell Emma.
(*She starts out.*)

CLARK

Don't wake that poor woman this late.

**MARY**

I don't think she's gone to bed yet. Besides, she loves doing just this sort of thing. And I haven't given her much chance lately. (*She starts out*) You run around the room and work up an appetite. (*She exits through arch. He walks around the room happily. Suddenly he notices her father's portrait. He turns on the switch that lights it and stands back, admiring it and taking on its quality.* MARY *returns and sees this*) You feel another attack of being debonair coming on?

**CLARK**

A very bad attack. (*She goes to a vase of carnations, breaks one off and puts it in his buttonhole deftly, then moves away. He strolls across the room and stops in front of the picture again*) That's damn good. Who did it?

**MARY**

Manya Capek.

**CLARK**

Oh, Jan Capek's sister.

**MARY**

Yes.

(MARY *lights a cigarette with obvious nervousness.*)

**CLARK**

Say, you're a little shaky. Is this my effect on you—I hope— or is something else the matter?

**MARY**

I didn't sleep well last night. (*She gives him a quick look*) I never do.

**CLARK**

Another area of agreement. Meet a fellow sufferer.
(*He sits on the couch beside her.*)

**MARY**

I can get to sleep all right but I'm usually awake from three to five.

**CLARK**

My hours are four to six. It's terrible. My doctor says more people commit suicide between those hours than any other. What do you do for it?

**MARY**

I've tried everything.

**CLARK**

So have I.

**MARY**

At first I used to call up my friends. Then, of course, I ran out of friends.

**CLARK**

Warm baths?

MARY

Hot milk?

CLARK

Cold baths?

MARY

I've had the best luck with music.

CLARK

It's no good for me.

MARY

You haven't tried the right kind of music. I always have some ready.
(*She has gone to the phonograph and turns on a record.*)

CLARK

I won't want to go to sleep now. (*He listens for a moment*) I see what you mean. (*Another pause*) Chopin?

MARY

Yes. (MARY *sits again. They both listen to the music*) Strauss is good, too.

CLARK

I get my Strausses mixed up.

MARY

Well, there's Richard.

CLARK

Let's see, there were two Johanns, weren't there?

MARY

Yes, and one Oscar.

CLARK

And Jack.

MARY

Jack?

CLARK

That's what I mean, you see. He's one of the R. H. Macy Strausses.

(*She gives him a reproachful smile. They listen quietly, stealing glances at each other. Then her mind obviously wanders. He is conscious of this. She picks up from the end table a small pad with its pencil, also her glasses, which she puts on.*)

MARY

Elliott—what was the name of that poem?

CLARK

Nina Simonova's?

MARY

Yes.

CLARK

I can't remember it. I'll find it and send it to you. (*She returns the pad and pencil to the table, then leans back, listening to the music.* CLARK *reaches over and removes her glasses, takes them to the desk. Then he comes back to the couch*) They say sleeplessness is the child of loneliness.

MARY

Do they?
    (*The telephone rings.*)

CLARK

Uncle Theodore! The hell with it!

MARY

It's my private telephone. I have to answer it. (*She rises and goes to the telephone.* CLARK *turns off the phonograph. Into telephone*) Hello . . . Hello, Sir Audley . . . No, I'm still up. As a matter of fact, Elliott Clark's here. We've been talking. (CLARK *realizes he is* de trop *and wanders up toward the arch, as if looking for a chance to leave the room*) Oh? Oh— just a minute. (*To* CLARK) Don't you want another drink?

CLARK

*Au contraire.*
> (*She gets the idea and points toward the bedroom door. He goes into the bedroom and shuts the door behind him.*)

MARY

(*Into phone*)

All right, I'm alone now . . . I am not worried about the toxicologist's report. It's this suspicion of each other. How could any one of us have done such a thing? We each gave our personal word of honor . . . No, I haven't seen the morning papers . . . You mean that's in the papers? That's pure invention and we both know it. I think it's most unfair . . . (CLARK *enters from bedroom*) . . . I'm very upset . . . Let me call you in the morning. Good night. (MARY *hangs up and turns on* CLARK) It's not easy to fight for the freedom of the press when American newspapers abuse it.

CLARK

Now what?

MARY

The latest report is that I've been in touch with the District Attorney's office in the Capek case. The inference is pretty plain that it was I who directed suspicion against the Russians.

CLARK

You're being a little too upset.

MARY

Aren't there times when you're ashamed of having been a newspaperman?

CLARK

I'm very proud of having been a newspaperman! I'm proud of the newsmen on radio and on television. I've spent my life with them. I know them pretty well—name me another group where so many can be trusted.

MARY

Trusted!

CLARK

We have a few bastards and psychopaths—so has every profession. But most of the newspapermen I know are holding back a great many stories they could use out of a sheer sense of decency.

MARY

That's a little hard for me to believe.

CLARK

All right. I'm going to give you an example. I've been sitting on a story for fourteen years. It's never been printed and it never will be. (*He takes a moment to put out his cigarette*) Fourteen years ago I was on a vacation in Switzerland. I was starting out to climb a mountain. There was a little village about halfway up the mountain. I stopped to do some drinking. I sat on the terrace of a pension and I saw on the balcony of one of the rooms a member of the staff of the Czechoslovakian foreign office and a young woman I recognized—the daughter of an American ambassador.

MARY

Your example was very well chosen.

CLARK

I chose it deliberately, Mary. (*He studies her*) I think you're in trouble, and if you are, I want to help you.

MARY

What makes you think so?

CLARK

No one could have spent this evening with you without knowing something was wrong. Let me help you, Mary.

MARY

Elliott—I . . .
(*She is silent.*)

CLARK

Did Jan Capek die in this apartment?

MARY

No!

#### EMMA

*(Offstage)*

Here it is! All ready! (EMMA *enters with a laden tray. She places the tray on the table in front of the couch*) I'll bet you've never tasted scrapple like this, Mr. Clark. I made it just yesterday. Now you two sit down and enjoy it. Eat it while it's hot . . . I used your Earl Grey tea . . .

#### MARY

Thank you, Emma. Good night.
    (EMMA *starts out.* MARY *rises.*)

#### EMMA

    *(She looks at them a little quizzically)*
Well—good night.

#### CLARK

Good night. (EMMA *exits. There is a pause while* CLARK *waits for* EMMA *to get out of earshot*) What was behind that rumor?

#### MARY

Why do you ask me?

#### CLARK

There's something wrong with the story of Capek's death and I think you're concerned in it. Whatever hurts you will hurt what you stand for. Whether you like it or not, you are the Prescott Proposals.

MARY

I didn't know you were that interested in them.
(*He takes her by the arms and turns her toward him.*)


CLARK

I'm interested in you, Mary. I can't let you be in trouble.
Tell me about it.


MARY

There's nothing I have to tell.
(*He releases her.*)


CLARK

You must know you can trust me. (*A pause*) I thought by
now you and I . . . (*She walks to the chair beside the desk and
sits*) Is that the way we stand? (*She doesn't answer.* CLARK *is
deeply hurt*) Very well—good night. (*He walks out.*)
(MARY *hears the door close and her head turns slightly
in its direction. She sits for a moment, then picks up
her glasses from the desk and puts them on. Then she
takes them off, looks at them, puts them back on the
desk and sits, disconsolate, as*


*The Curtain Falls*

# ACT THREE

# ACT THREE

SCENE: *The committee room.*

TIME: *Early the next afternoon.*

AT RISE: *The Committee is in session. All of the Committee members are present. The* PRECIS-WRITER *is recording the proceedings. Each member of the Committee has two experts seated behind him, except* DR. MASOUD, *who has one. Some of them have papers in their hands and on several occasions an expert will lean over and whisper to his delegate. The* CONFERENCE OFFICER *is seated at his desk. As the curtain rises,* D'ARCEAU *is in the middle of a speech.*

### D'ARCEAU

. . . It has become more and more evident that the Eastern governments have substituted obstruction for co-operation. That's all I have to say . . .

### SIR AUDLEY
*(With resigned patience)*

Any further discussion? *(Silence)* Very well. We shall now vote on whether item eleven shall become item six of the agenda. *(He pauses)* All in favor? (D'ARCEAU *and* MARY *raise their pencils*) Opposed? (DR. MASOUD *raises his pencil*) Two in favor. One opposed. Two abstaining. The motion is defeated. (*There is a pause, one or two of the delegates taking a deep breath*) I regret very much the atmosphere in which we are meeting today. Yesterday, meeting informally, in the space of a few minutes we decided on the first five items of the agenda. Today we have been in full formal session for almost two hours without being able to agree on item six. We are compelled to adjourn before three o'clock as Mr. Petrovsky is to address the General Assembly. Unless we come to some conclusions the day will be entirely wasted. We have already rejected as item six items formerly numbered seven, eight, nine, ten, eleven and twenty-seven. Is there a motion that item twelve now become item six of the agenda?

### PETROVSKY

I so move.

### BABICKA

I second.

### SIR AUDLEY

Is there any discussion? (MARY *holds up her pencil*) The representative of the United States.

### MARY

I shall have to vote against the motion. As I said at yesterday's meeting, I feel that the early items of the agenda should be the ones that give most promise of agreement.

# THE PRESCOTT PROPOSALS

Is there any further discussion? (*Silence*) All in favor? (PE-TROVSKY *and* BABICKA *raise their pencils*) Opposed? (MARY *and* D'ARCEAU *raise their pencils*) Two in favor. Two against. One abstaining. The motion is defeated. (PETROVSKY *raises his pencil*) The representative of the Soviet Union.


#### PETROVSKY

Mr. Chairman, it would be very advantageous if the early items of the agenda were those on which we could come to an agreement. It would be very pleasant if all the items were those upon which we could agree. My observation tells me there is a very simple way to achieve this. All that is necessary is that we who are here as representatives of other sovereign states approve of everything that is suggested by the distinguished representative of the United States of America.

(MARY *immediately raises her pencil.*)


#### SIR AUDLEY
(*Resigned*)
The representative of the United States.


#### MARY

I must protest that implication. The government of the United States has shown every desire to co-operate. There is at this table an empty chair. I think that chair is symbolic of my government's willingness to compromise. In previous circumstances that chair would have been occupied by a representative of China. I think it is indicative of my country's co-operation that that chair is at present empty.

SIR AUDLEY

Which only means that one fifth of the world's population
is not here represented!

PETROVSKY

Exactly!

BABICKA

The 400,000,000 people who are happily united under the
government of the Peoples Republic of China are without
representation in the United Nations. How can we call ourselves the United Nations when . . .

(SIR AUDLEY *raps.*)

SIR AUDLEY

I'm sorry. This is partly my fault. The subject of the status
of China is not pertinent to our discussions and I shall have
to rule it out of order. (*During the above the telephone lights
at the* CONFERENCE OFFICER's *desk have flashed. The* CON-
FERENCE OFFICER *has answered it and taken a sheet of paper
and a pencil and written something dictated to him over the
phone. At this point the* CONFERENCE OFFICER *goes to* MASOUD
*and hands him the note.* MASOUD *reads it*) I believe the time
has come when we must return to the spirit in which this Subcommittee was delegated its task. (SIR AUDLEY *turns and
speaks to one of his experts*) Let me have that report of the
Secretary-General.

(*The* EXPERT *digs into his own brief case and produces
the report, which he hands to* SIR AUDLEY. MASOUD *has
finished reading the note, smiles at* SIR AUDLEY *and
points to it.*)

142

# THE PRESCOTT PROPOSALS

MASOUD

Mr. Chairman, very good news.

*(Then, with a whispered word,* MASOUD *hands the paper to* D'ARCEAU, *who starts reading it.)*

SIR AUDLEY

To this point I wish to read an excerpt from the report of the Secretary-General, Mr. Hammarskjold, submitted August 3, 1953. (D'ARCEAU *has finished reading the note, smiles at* MASOUD *and passes it on to* MARY *with pleasant excitement. Again* SIR AUDLEY *notices this but starts reading:)* "As an instrument for conciliation, the United Nations provides a forum which should serve the members *less* for the voicing of complaints and *more* for the preservation of proposals furthering the common end. (MARY *turns to* D'ARCEAU *with a pleased look and a quick whisper.* SIR AUDLEY *holds out his right hand in anticipation of receiving the note.* MARY, *not noticing this, hands the note to one of the American* EXPERTS, *indicating it is to be passed along)* "The organization can grow in influence only insofar as the peoples of the world feel that what is brought out in its conference rooms . . . (*He realizes* MARY *has not handed him the note and wonders about it)* ". . . in its conference rooms represents an expression of the constructive will of the member nations to put the common international interest before national demands. (*At this point he sees the note being handed to* BABICKA *and realizes it has been passed behind him)* ". . . and insofar as they are given reason for confidence that the machinery of the international co-operation represented by the United Nations—(SIR AUDLEY *now sees the note being passed by* BABICKA *to* PETROVSKY)

". . . is an adequate means of reaching sound compromises, based on the charter between the interests involved." (*He looks up as* PETROVSKY *has finished reading the note*) And now may the chairman ask what the hell is going on?

### PETROVSKY

I shall read. (*He reads the note*) "The medical examiner's office reported today that no poison was found by the toxicologist in the examination of the body of Jan Capek, former Czechoslovakian delegate to the United Nations. The medical examiner's finding is that Mr. Capek died of a heart attack. This ends the official inquiry."

### SIR AUDLEY

Well, that settles that.

### D'ARCEAU

*L'affaire Capek, c'est finis!*

### MARY

Well, that's over. The whole thing should never have happened.

(PETROVSKY *holds up his pencil.*)

### SIR AUDLEY

The representative of the Soviet Union.

### PETROVSKY

Mr. Chairman, since this incident was used by the American newspapers to incite international hatreds I wish to propose a resolution which I urge be placed as item six on the agenda. In substance it would be something like this: That newspapers be forbidden to publish any unsubstantiated rumors that might lead to international tension.

(*Both* MASOUD *and* MARY *raise their pencils.*)


### SIR AUDLEY

The representative of the United States.


### MARY

(*Lowering her pencil*)
The representative of Pakistan wishes to speak.


### MASOUD

Thank you. The distinguished representative of the Soviet Union has offered a very interesting resolution. However, I hope he will consider an amendment. What I have in mind . . .

(D'ARCEAU *raises his pencil and speaks without waiting to be recognized.*)


### D'ARCEAU

Mr. Chairman, a point of order. It is against our procedure to consider an amendment unless the resolution to be amended is before us in writing. The distinguished representative of Pakistan should know we cannot possibly amend a proposal that has not yet been formulated.

145

SIR AUDLEY

The position of the representative of France is well taken. (PETROVSKY *raises his pencil*) The representative of the Soviet Union.

PETROVSKY

I shall have my resolution drafted and presented in writing at tomorrow morning's session.

SIR AUDLEY

Are you still proposing that it become item six?

PETROVSKY

I am.

SIR AUDLEY

That rather puts an end to the hope of accomplishing anything today.

(PETROVSKY *raises his pencil.* SIR AUDLEY *nods.*)

PETROVSKY

Mr. Chairman, it might be helpful before I draft my resolution to have the opinions of some of the other distinguished members of the Committee. Let us suppose that the rumors about the death of Mr. Capek were true—that he did indeed die in someone's apartment rather than in the automobile. Should the newspapers have been allowed to publish this as a rumor before corroborating evidence had been established?

I should like to hear from the distinguished representative of the United States.

MARY

My government's position is that there can be no restrictions of the freedom of the press. We have, of course, as most countries have, punitive laws against libel.

PETROVSKY

That, you tell me, is the position of Your Excellency's government. Would I be transgressing if I asked whether it would be Your Excellency's personal position?

(SIR AUDLEY *raps with his gavel.*)

MARY

You would be transgressing and it is my personal position.

(SIR AUDLEY *raps again.*)

PETROVSKY

May I hear from the distinguished representative of France?

D'ARCEAU

I can conceive of such a law in the Soviet Union and in any of the countries subservient to it. It would not be acceptable to my government and that would be my personal opinion, also, in case the distinguished representative of the Soviet Union wants to know.

(SIR AUDLEY *raps vigorously during the end of* D'AR-CEAU'S *speech.*)

SIR AUDLEY

We are here representing our governments. Any request for a personal opinion or any expression of one is shockingly out of order. (*He looks at his watch*) We still have ten minutes, but rather than spend that additional time not getting anywhere I suggest that we adjourn. (*The* EXPERTS *begin to pack up and strap their brief cases. Some of them rise, then later resume their seats*) However, before any motion is made to adjourn I should like to call this to the Committee's attention. The other committees which have been created to deal with the Prescott Proposals—the Subcommittee on disarmament, the Subcommittee on freedom of movement, all the others—have agreed on their agenda and are making excellent progress. I hope that beginning tomorrow we shall profit by their example.

D'ARCEAU

I move we adjourn.

MASOUD

I second the motion.

SIR AUDLEY

All in favor? (*They all raise their pencils*) Carried. We meet here tomorrow at eleven o'clock.

> (*There is a general movement as the* EXPERTS *rise to their feet, and start to exit. One English* EXPERT *helps* SIR AUDLEY *pack his papers and the same aid is given to* D'ARCEAU. PETROVSKY *and one of his* EXPERTS *confer briefly before the* EXPERT *exits.* BABICKA *is one of the*

*first to exit. The* CONFERENCE OFFICER *replaces some of the chairs against the wall and then exits.* MASOUD *has been packing his brief case very deliberately.* SIR AUD-LEY *takes* MARY'S *chair and confers with* D'ARCEAU *inaudibly.* MARY *goes to the* CONFERENCE OFFICER'S *desk to return a document, then crosses right to speak to one of the American* EXPERTS *down right.*)

MARY

Will you have five copies made of this, please? (*She is about to hand him a paper, when she sees* KATHLEEN, *who has entered carrying a brief case*) Oh, never mind. Here's Miss Murray. Kathleen, will you have five copies made of this? I'll meet you at the office later.

(*She hands* KATHLEEN *the paper. All of the* AIDES *and the* CONFERENCE OFFICER *have now left the room.*)

KATHLEEN

Mrs. Prescott, Elliott Clark is waiting in the corridor for you.

MARY

Please tell him I can't see him.

KATHLEEN

He wants to talk to you.

MARY

Just tell him there's nothing I have to say to him.

KATHLEEN

He told me you might say that. He said to tell you that doesn't matter—that his professional perspective is entirely gone, whatever that means.


MARY

It's no use, Kathleen. Please tell him I can't see him.


KATHLEEN

Very well.

(MARY *turns away. She meets* PETROVSKY *as he is leaving the table. He stops and speaks to her. As they talk,* KATHLEEN *looks at the paper* MARY *has given her, zips open her large leather envelope and puts it in.*)


PETROVSKY

That was good news about the autopsy.


MARY

At least there'll be no more of it in the newspapers.


PETROVSKY

I am happy especially for you. You have been under a great strain.


MARY

We all have.

PETROVSKY

But it is you for whom I am most pleased. Now you can smile again.

MARY

Thank you. (*He smiles at her, bows and starts for the* CON-FERENCE OFFICER'S *desk. She watches him as he crosses. At this moment,* KATHLEEN *starts out.* MARY *sees her*) Just a minute, Kathleen!

> (KATHLEEN *turns and comes back.* PETROVSKY *goes to the telephone, getting there just as* DR. MASOUD *has reached it.*)

MASOUD

You wish to use the telephone? Please do.
> (PETROVSKY *dials.*)

PETROVSKY

Thank you. I am pressed for time. There is a crisis at the school for the children of the Russian staff. It must be settled before I go to the floor.

MASOUD

I can use the telephone in the lounge.

MARY

(*To* KATHLEEN)
Wait for me in the corridor—and ask Mr. Clark to wait, too.

KATHLEEN

Yes, Mrs. Prescott.
(*She goes.* DR. MASOUD *has started for the door.*)

PETROVSKY

(*Into the telephone, in Russian*)
Petrovsky. Get me Malinin.

MARY

Dr. Masoud, do you mind staying for a moment? (*He stops.*
SIR AUDLEY *and* D'ARCEAU *are about to leave.* MARY *speaks to
them*) Paul-Emile, Sir Audley, I want to speak to all of you
as soon as Mr. Petrovsky is free.

PETROVSKY

(*Into telephone*)
Find him and have him call me here in the committee
room. (*He hangs up and turns to* MARY) They will call me.
Yes?

MARY

I have a favor to ask all of you. Well, favor is not the word
—it goes much deeper than that.

SIR AUDLEY

What is it, Mary? What can we do for you?

MARY

This is difficult for me—very difficult. We all pledged our word the circumstances of Jan Capek's death would never be revealed. Now that the danger has passed—I want you to release me from my promise.

D'ARCEAU

Mary, that's impossible! We're all deeply involved!

MARY

I want permission to tell the truth to one person only.

D'ARCEAU

Just a minute, Mary.

MARY

The person I wish to tell, I can assure you, is as trustworthy as any of us. It will never go further.

PETROVSKY

We have all given our word.

MARY

(*With spirit*)

I have to remind you—I have to remind everyone in this room—someone has already broken his word. Otherwise there would have been no call to the District Attorney's office.

SIR AUDLEY

Mary, why do you ask this?

MARY

It's entirely a personal matter—but it's desperately important to me. That's why I beg you to give your consent.

MASOUD

But if anything further were to be revealed we would all be in a serious position. May I ask—is this someone we know?

MARY

Yes.

MASOUD

Perhaps if you were to tell us the name . . .
(*There is a pause.*)

MARY

It's—it's Elliott Clark.

SIR AUDLEY

I must say he's very well thought of, but upon my soul, Mary . . .

D'ARCEAU

Yes. He is a man I have trusted. But this goes beyond . . .
(*The lights are flashing on the telephone.*)

PETROVSKY

Our pledge cannot be broken without everyone agreeing, and I will never agree. (*He picks up the telephone and begins to talk rapidly in Russian, then after a glance at the others switches into Uzbec dialect*) Malinin? The Committee meeting has just adjourned. Tell Moscow I will telephone as soon as I have finished addressing the General Assembly. The scheme is working beautifully. They are fighting among themselves . . . (MASOUD *is about to start toward* MARY *when something arrests him. He turns and listens attentively to* PETROVSKY's *telephone conversation, unobserved by* PETROVSKY) They suspect each other exactly as we planned . . . Something new has just come up which has split them even further. It is possible they may save us from making the final disclosure . . . Yes . . . I will include that. Good-bye.

> (*He hangs up.* MARY *lets herself down into a chair.* SIR AUDLEY *and* D'ARCEAU *go over to her. They continue to talk to her somewhat inaudibly, as* PETROVSKY *makes some notes.*)

MASOUD

(*Quietly to* PETROVSKY)
You were able to settle the crisis at the children's school?

PETROVSKY

Yes, thank you. The education of the young is very important.

MASOUD

Yes, it is most important. (*To the others*) I have always regretted that when I was young I was not taught to speak and understand pure Russian. Unfortunately, my tutor came from Turkestan. So I understand only the Uzbec dialect. (PETROV-SKY *drops his pencil, turns, rises and steps toward* MASOUD, *glaring at him angrily. To the others*) I have something to tell you. It was Petrovsky who made the anonymous telephone call. He just revealed this unmistakably.

PETROVSKY

So! What of it?

SIR AUDLEY

Petrovsky!

MASOUD

He has broken his pledge. I feel we are no longer held to ours.

PETROVSKY

What you feel I do not care.

SIR AUDLEY

Mary, I think you are entitled to tell Mr. Clark.
(PETROVSKY *sits and dials on the telephone.* MARY *has opened the door. She speaks through it.*)

MARY

Would you ask Mr. Clark to step in here, please?
(*She returns immediately toward the others.*)

156

D'ARCEAU

(*To* MASOUD)

You understood all those telephone calls and did not tell us?

MASOUD

It was not until now that I was sure.
(PETROVSKY, *in Russian, barks an order over the telephone, then waits.*)

PETROVSKY

Get me Smirnoff! *Smirnoff!* I must talk to him immediately.

MARY

(*To* MASOUD)

Dr. Masoud, you must have known we suspected you. (MASOUD *nods*) Why did you let us?

MASOUD

You know the Russian policy.

D'ARCEAU

What policy?

MASOUD

To spread distrust among the United States, France and England. That was Mr. Petrovsky's purpose. I thought it better for you to suspect me than to suspect each other.
(MARY *puts her hand on his arm, her expression revealing her gratitude.* CLARK *enters.*)

157

#### CLARK

Yes, Mrs. Prescott?

#### MARY

Last night there was something I wanted to tell you but couldn't. Now I'm free to.

(PETROVSKY *hangs up and rises.*)

#### PETROVSKY

Mrs. Prescott—I warn you—you are not free!

#### MARY

(*To* PETROVSKY)

Yes. I am free! (*She turns to* CLARK) Elliott, Jan Capek did die in my apartment. He came there because . . .

#### PETROVSKY

Very well, Mrs. Prescott, now you have told him. In three minutes I shall be before the General Assembly. I will tell them! I will tell the world!

(D'ARCEAU *and* SIR AUDLEY *speak simultaneously.*)

#### D'ARCEAU

*Mais c'est fou. C'est impossible que vous faissez une chose pareille.*

#### SIR AUDLEY

You couldn't do that—you couldn't possibly do that!

PETROVSKY

Yes? Listen to my speech. Come into the assembly and listen to me, all of you. (*To* CLARK) You will find out—everyone will find out—how much freedom of the press means to her—to this committee.

SIR AUDLEY

That's monstrous!

D'ARCEAU

You gave us your word.

SIR AUDLEY

Your personal word of honor!

PETROVSKY

My honor is the honor of the Communist Party. There is no such thing as personal honor.

SIR AUDLEY

You can't believe that.

PETROVSKY

Wait and see.

SIR AUDLEY

Do you realize what this would do to the United Nations?

D'ARCEAU

And you must know it would destroy Mrs. Prescott.

PETROVSKY

(*Deliberately*)

Yes, I do know. And it will give me great happiness!
(*He starts for the door.*)

CLARK

(*Angrily*)

Did it give you happiness to destroy Nina Simonova?
(PETROVSKY *stops, turns slowly toward* CLARK *and, livid with anger, takes a step toward him, stops, draws himself up, looks from* CLARK *to* MARY *and back, as if he now had added incentive to destroy them both, and strides out.* SIR AUDLEY *goes immediately to the telephone and dials a number.*)

D'ARCEAU

Swine! (*He sinks into a chair*) Well, this is the end of all of us.
(MARY *slowly sits and* CLARK *goes to her side.*)

SIR AUDLEY

Not for a moment! We're in a fight—let's fight!

D'ARCEAU

I hope they will let me be at least consul at San Francisco.

# THE PRESCOTT PROPOSALS

SIR AUDLEY

(*Into telephone*)

Hello? . . . That you, Herbert? . . . Sir Audley . . . See here, Herbert, Petrovsky is about to address the General Assembly. I want you to get word to the President immediately that if he mentions any member of this Committee by name, I insist on the right to answer him immediately. Make sure of this, Herbert. I shall be in my seat. I'm going there now. (*He hangs up*) Come along, Paul-Emile. I'll need your support.

D'ARCEAU

It's not every man who can attend his own funeral.

(D'ARCEAU *goes slowly to the door.* SIR AUDLEY *comes down to* CLARK.)

SIR AUDLEY

(*To* CLARK)

You stay with Mary.

MARY

No. I must be there.

CLARK

Mary, that would just serve his purpose.

SIR AUDLEY

(*To* CLARK, *indicating a dial on the wall*)

You can listen from here.

(SIR AUDLEY *and* D'ARCEAU *exit.*)

MASOUD

Mrs. Prescott, I watched Petrovsky's face when he turned from that door. He had seen a ghost. Be of good courage.
(MASOUD *exits.*)

CLARK

You feel you must hear it?

MARY

Oh, yes. (*She looks up at him*) I'm glad you're here.
(CLARK *goes to the wall and turns the dial. We hear an* ANNOUNCER'S VOICE *over a loud-speaker.*)

ANNOUNCER'S VOICE

. . . an expectant buzz and murmur as the delegates wait to hear Mr. Petrovsky. The President is about to speak.

PRESIDENT'S VOICE

The representative of the Soviet Union.

ANNOUNCER'S VOICE

Mr. Petrovsky has reached the lectern, and now I shall turn you over to the interpreter . . .
(*The map on the back wall becomes transparent and through it we see* PETROVSKY *at the lectern of the General Assembly. We hear* PETROVSKY'S *voice, speaking in Russian. This quickly fades under the voice of the* IN-

TERPRETER, *speaking English.* MARY *moves restlessly around the room.* CLARK *is immobile and silent, watching her.*)

#### INTERPRETER'S VOICE

Madame President and Members of the General Assembly: I come before you today because the American people are being misinformed by the capitalistic American press. I have information that is as yet unknown even to members of this distinguished assembly. I can report to you today how the government of the United States and its representatives deceive the American people through their lying newspapers. You have all heard, I presume, the report of the Medical Examiner in the recent unfortunate death of Jan Capek, delegate from Czechoslovakia to the United Nations. The capitalist American press has been full of vicious rumors reflecting on Czechoslovakia and the Soviet Union. One of these rumors, which has appeared in print, was that Delegate Capek died in the apartment of an official high in the United Nations. Other rumors, not printed, even named this official. And that brings me to the distinguished representative of the United States, Mrs. Prescott . . . (MARY *starts to put her hands to her ears*) Mrs. *Nina* Prescott!

(MARY'S *hands stop beside her ears.* CLARK *looks sharply in the direction of the* INTERPRETER'S VOICE.)

#### CLARK

Nina . . .?

(*At the lectern, we see* PETROVSKY *catch himself in shock, then shout almost hysterically.*)

INTERPRETER'S VOICE

Mrs. *Mary* Prescott!

> (PETROVSKY *seizes the edges of the lectern and stands there, shaken. Then he wipes his hands across his eyes, as if trying to wipe away a picture.*)

ANNOUNCER'S VOICE

Mr. Petrovsky seems ill. It is not like him ever to hesitate. I will turn you back to the interpreter.

> (PETROVSKY *gradually regains a sober control and speaks calmly and deliberately.*)

INTERPRETER'S VOICE

Jan Capek died exactly as reported—exactly as you have been told that he died by the distinguished representative of the United Kingdom. He died of a heart attack in the car of the British Ambassador. Every investigation we have made confirms this fact. Every rumor to the contrary printed by the venal American press is a lie. It is well known that the American capitalists own and control the press ... (PETROVSKY *is struggling to regain his control. He tries to speak again*) It is well known ...

> (PETROVSKY *stops abruptly, unable to continue, and we see him turn to leave the lectern. The lights fade out behind the map.* MARY *has collapsed into a chair.* ELLIOTT *goes to her and puts his hands on her shoulders. She takes one of his hands and holds it against her cheek.*)

164

###### ANNOUNCER'S VOICE

Mr. Petrovsky has ended his speech abruptly and is leaving the rostrum. We do not know what has happened. We will try to find out and report it to you in our continuing coverage of the United Nations in session.

> (*There is a murmur over the loud-speaker.* SIR AUDLEY *bursts into the room.*)

###### SIR AUDLEY

Did you hear? Now he *has* told the world. He can never go back on that story!

###### CLARK

Yes, we heard. What will happen to him now?

###### SIR AUDLEY

He'll be recalled, and then . . .

> (*He shrugs.* D'ARCEAU *enters.*)

###### D'ARCEAU

He has finished! There is no longer danger!

> (*Suddenly we hear clearly over the loudspeaker* **the** *voice of the* PRESIDENT.)

###### PRESIDENT'S VOICE

The representative of the United Kingdom.

###### SIR AUDLEY

> (*Startled*)

Good Lord! That's me! (*He starts for the door, then turns to* D'ARCEAU) There's nothing for me to say!

### D'ARCEAU

You are at your most brilliant when you have nothing to say!

(SIR AUDLEY *and* D'ARCEAU *start out, passing* PETROVSKY *as they leave.* PETROVSKY *starts to pack his brief case.* MARY *and* CLARK *watch him. Then over the loudspeaker we hear* SIR AUDLEY'S *voice.*)

### SIR AUDLEY'S VOICE

Madame President, members of the General Assembly: The distinguished representative of the Soviet Union doesn't seem to believe . . .

(PETROVSKY *goes to the wall, turns the knob, and all is silent.* PETROVSKY *returns to his brief case.*)

### MARY

Mr. Petrovsky, I want to thank you.

### PETROVSKY

For what? Because I did not expose you? (*Still shaken*) Do not thank me. I—I was not myself.

### MARY

You're wrong. For a moment, you *were* yourself. You were human. You were a Russian—not a Communist. That's why I know what you stand for has to lose.

PETROVSKY

We will never lose. We are not afraid of your atomic bombs. They can not defeat Communism.

(*He starts for the door.*)

MARY

It's the human spirit that will defeat Communism, Mr. Petrovsky. What happened inside you today will someday happen inside Russia.

PETROVSKY

(*Defiantly*)

We shall see!

MARY

(*Confidently*)

Yes—you will see. (PETROVSKY *exits*) Do you see, Elliott?

CLARK

Yes, Mary. I see. But it may take generations.

MARY

It may take a hundred years. But I know now—no iron curtain can divide the human race. I've seen a spark, Elliott . . . (KATHLEEN *enters*) A tiny, tiny spark in a dark world. . . .

KATHLEEN

Mrs. Prescott, I hate to interrupt you, but Ambassador Lodge is about to make a speech.

MARY

*(She glances wryly toward* ELLIOTT)

So was I.

KATHLEEN

He's speaking on the Prescott Proposals and you should be in your seat.

MARY

I'll be right there, Kathleen.

(KATHLEEN *exits.* MARY *crosses right and picks up her fur piece and gloves.*)

CLARK

When am I going to see you again?

MARY

I haven't the slightest idea!

CLARK

How about dinner tonight? Unless it's dangerous for you to be seen too much with me.

MARY

Well, it may be dangerous for you.

CLARK

For me?

MARY

Yes. You see, I've become famous for proposals!

(*She exits swiftly.*)

**Curtain**

# About the authors

THE COMBINATION of Howard Lindsay and Russel Crouse is one of the most prominent and successful collaborations in the theatre today. Between them they have been active in every department of the theatre: producing, acting, directing and even press agentry.

Lindsay and Crouse met as a writing partnership for the book of the musical hit, *Anything Goes* (1934). Since then their successes have included *Life with Father, Call Me Madam, Remains to Be Seen* and the 1945 Pulitzer Prize-winning *State of the Nation*.

Mr. Crouse is a former newspaperman and columnist. Mr. Lindsay is currently chairman of the Council of the Living Theatre.